DEVON
VILLAINS

ROGUES,
RASCALS
AND
REPROBATES

The Man that Broke the Bank at Monte Carlo.

I've just got here, through Paris, from the sunny
    southern shore,
    I to Monte Carlo went, just to raise my winter's
      rent;
Dame Fortune smil'd upon me as she'd never done
    before,
    And I've now such lots of money, I'm a gent,
    Yes, now I've such lots of money, I'm a gent.

Chorus.

    As I walk along the Bois Boolong,
    With an independent air,
    You can hear the girls declare—
    He must be a millionaire.
    You can hear them sigh
    And wish to die,
    You can see them wink the other eye
    At the man who broke the bank at Monte Carlo.

I stay in doors till after lunch, and then my daily
    walk,
    To the great Triumphal Arch is one grand triumphal
      march,
Observed by each observer with the keenness of a
    hawk,
    I'm a mass of money, linen, silk, and starch.
    I'm a mass of money, linen, silk, and starch.

I patronised the tables at the Monte Carlo hell,
    Till they hadn't got a sou for a Christian or a Jew;
I then flew off to Paris for the charms of mad'moiselle,
    Who's the loadstone of my heart—what can I do
    When with twenty tongues she swears that she'll
      be true?

DEVON VILLAINS

ROGUES, RASCALS AND REPROBATES

MIKE HOLGATE

Frontispiece: Overleaf is a song sheet lauding the gambling exploits of Plymouth fraudster Charles De Ville Wells (written before he lost every penny of his investor's money at the casino tables in Monte Carlo).

First published 2011

The History Press
The Mill, Brimscombe Port
Stroud, Gloucestershire, GL5 2QG
www.thehistorypress.co.uk

© Mike Holgate, 2011

The right of Mike Holgate to be identified as the Author
of this work has been asserted in accordance with the
Copyrights, Designs and Patents Act 1988.

British Library Cataloguing in Publication Data.
A catalogue record for this book is available from the British Library.

ISBN 978 0 7524 6074 1

Typesetting and origination by The History Press
Printed in Great Britain
Manufacturing managed by Jellyfish Print Solutions Ltd

Contents

About the Author

Since graduating from Plymouth University in 1988, Mike Holgate has combined three careers as a librarian, entertainer and author. The singer-songwriter performs talks-cum-concerts on historical subjects inspired by the titles of his many books including: *Devon Ghosts and Legends*; *The Man They Could Not Hang*; *Murder & Mystery on the Great Western Railway*; *Devon: Murder & Crime*; *Jack the Ripper: The Celebrity Suspects*; *Agatha Christie's True Crime Inspirations* and, of course, *Devon Villains*. His research on the county's most infamous criminal John Lee was used by Granada Television for the series *In Suspicious Circumstances* in 1995 and a BBC Radio Devon play, *A Shadow of Doubt: The Story of the Man They Couldn't Hang* in 2008.

Acknowledgements

The author would like to express his appreciation for access to archive material, books, newspapers and online resources available at the John Pike Local Studies Library, Torquay; Naval and Local Studies Library, Plymouth; and the West Country Studies Library, Exeter.

Illustrations

Supplementing the author's own collection, the majority of the illustrations in this book have been obtained from the Local Studies collection at Torquay Library containing prints, postcards, photographs, antiquarian books, journals and periodicals.

Introduction

Legendary North Devon highwayman Tom Faggus (featured in the classic novel *Lorna Doone*), East Devon smuggler Jack Rattenbury (dubbed 'The Rob Roy of the West'), South Devon murderer John Lee (famed as 'The Man They Could Not Hang') and West Devon fraudster Charles De Ville Wells – immortalised for his gambling exploits in the music hall song 'The Man Who Broke the Bank at Monte Carlo' – are featured among the traitors, pirates, smugglers, robbers, fraudsters and killers in this veritable who's who of the county's best-loved rogues and most notorious villains. From so-called beheaded 'traitors' Lady Jane Grey and Sir Walter Raleigh to daring train robbers Henry Poole and Bruce Reynolds, it's amazing how many of these men and women, deemed to have broken the law of the land, captured the public imagination, often commanding sympathy and admiration for their nefarious acts. Many of the wrongdoers included in this book have also been lauded in traditional ballads, poetry or popular song and I would like to preface their stories with a rhyming tribute of my own:

> Dedicated to the reprobates,
> traitors, rogues and felons,
> who are featured in this book
> of infamous 'Devon Villains'.

Mike Holgate, 2011

9

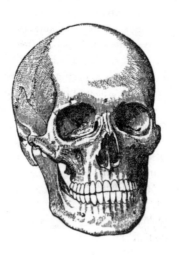

Chapter One

Murderers

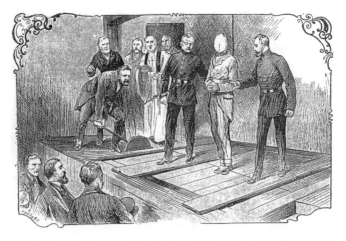

William De Tracey, John Lee, Charlotte Winsor, Herbert Rowse Armstrong, Harry Grant and Robert Hichen were all found guilty of committing capital charges, although all but one escaped the death penalty.

William De Tracy: The Assassination of Thomas Becket

Where is Becket, the traitor to the King?
Where is Becket, the meddling priest?
Come down Daniel to the lion's den,
Come down Daniel and join in the feast.

From verse drama *Murder in the Cathedral* by T.S. Eliot.

On Christmas Day 1170, the long-standing feud between Henry II and the Archbishop of Canterbury, Thomas Becket, finally erupted when news reached the king at court in France that Becket, recently reinstated after spending six years in exile, had excommunicated the bishops who had officiated at Henry's coronation during his absence and, according to them, was ready to 'tear the crown from the young king's head'. The monarch was enraged: 'What a pack of fools and cowards have I nourished in my household,' he cried, 'that not one of them will avenge me of this turbulent priest.'

William de Tracy, Reginald FitzUrse, Hugh de Murville, and Richard le Breton were stung into action by this outburst and immediately set sail for England, believing they had the king's blessing. The four knights rode to Canterbury, and when they entered the archbishop's chamber, Sir William de Tracy was the only one whom Thomas recognised and greeted by name. A ferocious argument ensued and the knights left to arm themselves and returned to the cathedral an hour later to carry out their vow to slay Becket. Tracy strode forward and warned, 'Flee! Thou art death's man', but was seized by the archbishop, who flung him aside. Several sword blows then rained down on the defenceless churchman and Tracy struck the fatal blow – which sliced off the crown of Becket's head, causing his brains to spill out onto the floor.

Becket's death sealed the self-fulfilling prophesy he had made when first offered the post by his former friend Henry: 'Should God permit me to be Archbishop I should lose your majesty's favour'. Their quarrels had stemmed from the issue of whether the State or Church should have jurisdiction in spiritual

The assassination of Thomas Becket.

matters, particularly in the case of a lawbreaking cleric's right to be tried in church courts rather than by the state. The murder provoked great indignation across Europe and miracles reportedly occurred to pilgrims visiting Becket's tomb. In 1173, the pope canonised Thomas, and King Henry was forced to visit Canterbury to pay penance; he was ceremoniously whipped by monks as he left the abbey. Immediately after the murder, William de Tracy returned to his own diocese in Devon and made a confession to Bishop Bartholomew of Exeter, then surrendered himself to the pope's mercy. He and his fellow conspirators were ordered to spend fourteen years with the Templars and adher to a lifelong penance of fasting and prayer. Tracy set out for the Holy Land in 1173, but, according to a contemporary report, got no further than Cosenza in Sicily. There he contracted a terrible wasting disease and died in agony, tearing away the decaying flesh from his body whilst praying incessantly for forgiveness from Saint Thomas. On his deathbed he made out a charter granting his Devon manor of Doccombe to the chapter of Canterbury, 'for the love of God, the salvation of his own soul and his ancestors' souls, and for the love of the blessed Thomas, archbishop and martyr, of venerable memory'.

Bovey Tracey parish church of St Peter, Paul and Thomas of Canterbury.

The de Tracy family hailed from the Norman village of Traci near Bayeaux. The family seat in Devon was located at Morthoe, and it seems probable that Henry de Tracy was granted the Barony of Barnstaple during the reign of Henry II's predecessor, King Stephen. William de Tracy's pedigree is uncertain but there is a compelling theory that his grandfather was sired by Henry I (who publicly acknowledged only twenty of his numerous illegitimate offspring). Therefore, this branch of the de Tracy family took the mother's name and held the Baronies of Woollacombe and Bradninch. Following the murder of Thomas Becket, all members of the de Tracy family felt shamed and undertook charitable work in the county to atone for the wrongdoing.

Despite the fact that there is no evidence that Thomas Becket ever visited Devon, there is an intriguing myth associated with William de Tracy's motives for taking part in the assassination. The tale relates that the archbishop visited Buckfast Abbey and later journeyed to Bovey Tracey where he was entertained by de Tracy and his wife. Later, while her husband was attending King Henry's court in France, Lady de Tracy invited the churchman to counsel her on religious matters, but this was misconstrued by Sir William (who believed these liaisons were evidence of an affair). After the grim deed, Sir William retreated to Morthoe and sent for his wife, who was horrified to learn of her husband's misguided jealousy. The shock of Becket's death caused her to go into labour and the couple's son was stillborn. Filled with remorse for doubting the integrity of Lady de Tracy and Sir Thomas, William decided to erect churches dedicated to the memory of the saint at Morthoe, Barnstaple and Bovey Tracey.

According to legend, William de Tracy broke his sword as a gesture of repentance and threw it into the River Bovey. Many centuries later, such a weapon was retrieved from the water and restored by welding the pieces together. It was put on permanent display at The Riverside Hotel. As a constant reminder to Devonians of William de Tracy's treachery, it is said that the ghost of St Thomas Becket gallops through the village of Lapford on his way to Nymet Tracey at midnight on the anniversary of his death.

Charlotte Winsor: The Wholesale Child Murderess

What must this wretches' feelings be,
As the babes at her did smile.
She would kiss them tenderly,
With murder lurking on her mind.

Adapted from contemporary broadsheet ballad.

Distinguished author Charles Dickens commented on the extraordinary case of convicted child murderer Charlotte Winsor: 'It has been the destiny of that weird old woman to give more trouble, to waste more time and money, and to sit longer in courts of justice, than any other criminal of ancient or modern times. To bring down the excellent [hangman] Calcraft on three fruitless errands to Exeter; to have her scaffold thrice built and her grave thrice dug... in the solution of Hamlet's problem "To be or not to be" this was a "simple coming in for one woman"'.

At Torquay, in February 1865, a man was walking along a lane near Torre Railway Station when he made a horrific discovery. Lying in the snow was what appeared to be a discarded parcel,

Hangman William Calcraft was thwarted three times.

but closer examination revealed that it was in fact the body of a baby boy wrapped in newspaper. The police checked church records for recent baptisms and called upon parents to account for the whereabouts of their newborn sons. Their enquiries led them to unmarried servant Mary Jane Harris, whose relationship with a Farmer Nichols had resulted in the birth of Thomas Edwin Gibson Harris in October 1864. The twenty-three-year-old mother lied to the police, claiming that her child was being cared for by her aunt at Morehampstead. When Mary Harris and her son's former childminder, Charlotte Winsor, were taken in for questioning, Winsor passed a finger across her throat as a warning to Harris, who then nervously asked a police official, 'If I tell the truth, shall I be hung?' Both women denied that the body belonged to baby Thomas and the surgeon who carried out a post-mortem testified at the inquest that death was consistent with either suffocation or exposure. Harris and Winsor were arrested and indicted for infanticide, but at their trial, held at Exeter Castle, the pair pleaded their innocence and the jury failed to reach a verdict after deliberating for five hours. The judge discharged them at midnight on a Saturday as his presence was required at the forthcoming Bodmin Assizes on the following Monday morning. There was a sensational development at the re-trial, when Mary Jane Harris was persuaded to save her own neck – and subsequently released

Charlotte Winsor and her 'baby farm'.

when no case was offered against her by the prosecution – after she agreed to turn Queen's evidence against her co-defendant, Winsor.

According to the testimony of Harris, Charlotte Winsor, aged forty-five, boasted of killing several children, in the certain belief that she was 'doing good' by disposing of unwanted children. She told the witness, 'I will help anyone that will never split upon me. I will do whatever lays in my power for your child. Give me £5 and I will do away with the child. I'll put them all by for thee if thee hast forty'. The witness admitted that she stood by and allowed the death of her son to occur when the 'baby-farmer' took Thomas into a bedroom and smothered the infant.

Under cross-examination, Mary Harris denied that Winsor had prevented her from feeding rat poison placed on sugar candy to her child, or stopped her from immersing her tot's head in a bowl of water in an attempt to drown him. Despite no other charges being laid against her, Winsor was dubbed the 'wholesale child murderess' by the press and sentenced to death. However, she was spared from the hangman's rope on a legal technicality. The judge of the original trial had contravened a rule by discharging the jury without the consent of the accused, thereby, in the view of the accused woman's counsel, rendering the second trial illegal. Following protracted legal proceedings the appeal was overruled, but as the prisoner had waited a year for this decision, during which period she had endured the

Execution of Mrs. Winsor
At Exeter,
For the barbarous murder of Mary Jane Harris's Child

A premature report of the killer's death.

'mental anguish' of imminent execution on three occasions, Queen Victoria exercised the royal prerogative of mercy and the death penalty was commuted to life-imprisonment. During her year-long tenancy of the death cell, Winsor made a written statement admitting complicity in the crime, whilst maintaining that it was the mother who committed the actual deed. The convicted child killer was incarcerated for almost thirty years for her heinous crime, remaining in prison until her death in 1894.

At the first appointed execution of the notorious 'baby farmer', a souvenir broadsheet was prematurely published in advance of the capital punishment that did not take place:

'At the usual hour this morning Mrs Winsor expiated her crime on the gallows. Thousands assembled in front of the gaol at a very early hour, and many had walked all night to see the execution. Great commotion prevailed and it was evident that the crowd viewed the execution of a woman as a novelty, while they freely discussed the fiendish nature of the culprit, and expressed their total abhorrence of one who could make a business of murdering illegitimate offsprings. The horrible nature of the woman's crime… so shocked the better feelings of humanity, that when culprit and hangman stood side by side a fearful yell rose from the assembled crowd, and the excitement only ceased when the culprit, who struggled but little, ceased to exist.'

John Lee: The Man They Could Not Hang

The death of John Lee was not meant to be,
His life they could not take away.
Three times to the gallows they brought him,
But he survived to tell the tale.

From contemporary broadsheet ballad.

John Lee was born in the village of Abbotskerswell, situated midway between the seaside resort of Torquay and the market town of Newton Abbot. He joined the navy in 1879 and received an award, the Admiralty prize for general progress, whilst on the training ship HMS *Implacable*, which was based at Devonport, Plymouth. However, his chosen career was ended by a serious bout of pneumonia and he was invalided out of the service in 1882.

Despondently returning to South Devon, he then made a disastrous career move, accepting the position of footman to Colonel Brownlow at his Torquay villa, Ridgehill. Wealthy spinster Emma Keyse, for whom Lee had worked as the 'boy' before joining the navy, arranged the interview. She thought highly of Lee, but her faith was shaken when he stole several items of silver from his new master and was arrested attempting to pawn them in Devonport. Serving six months' hard labour in Exeter Prison, Lee was given a chance to redeem his character when Miss Keyse offered him employment upon his release on New Year's Day, 1884. She owned a large estate in Babbacombe and resided at The Glen, a fine villa on the beach where she had received visits from three future monarchs: Queen Victoria, George V and Edward VII.

In the early hours of the morning on Saturday, 15 November 1884, local fishermen and coastguardsmen were urgently summoned to The Glen to fight a fire that was sweeping through the house. When the flames were quelled, the smouldering body of Miss Keyse was found on the floor in the lounge, but it soon became evident that she had been killed before the blaze with blows to the head dealt with a blunt instrument. Also, every drop of blood had drained from her body when her throat was cut through to the vertebrae with a knife. The police investigation discovered no

The Babbacombe Murder.   John Lee.

signs of a break-in and after questioning the victim's three female servants; suspicion therefore soon fell on 'the only man in the house' – John Lee. The twenty-year-old servant slept on a pull-down bed in the pantry only 9ft from where the victim had been attacked, and the murderer would have had to squeeze past the end of the bed to reach the paraffin which had been used to start the blaze. His claim that he was a heavy sleeper and had heard nothing was dismissed by the police, and the fact that he had been discontented and involved in heated arguments with his employer led to his arrest.

Lee's half-sister Elizabeth Harris was the cook at The Glen and gave damning evidence that the accused had been angry about receiving a reduction in his wages and threatened to have his revenge. She alleged that once, when his work was criticised, he threatened to 'push the old lady off a cliff', while on another occasion he vowed to 'level the place to ashes' and watch it burn from the top of the hill. The jury took little more than half an hour to return a 'guilty' verdict. In passing sentence of death, the judge commented on the prisoner's calm demeanour during the proceedings. At this point, the prisoner stunned the court by leaning forward in the dock and replying: 'My Lord, the reason why I am so calm is because I trust in my Lord, who knows I am innocent'.

On Monday, 23 February 1885, the most infamous event in the history of capital punishment took place on the scaffold at

Exeter Prison. The executioner, James Berry, quickly pinioned the condemned man, drew a white cap over his head, and then tightened the noose around his neck, before pulling a lever to activate the 'drop' – then gasped in amazement as the trap door merely sagged two inches, leaving the prisoner precariously suspended between life and death! 'Quick, stamp on it!' he shouted to the warders.

Distressing scenes followed as desperate efforts were made to force the trap open. The warders jumped on the doors – and risked falling into the pit with the prisoner had they been successful – but after several minutes, the bewildered prisoner was led to one side, while the apparatus was tested and found to work perfectly. Visibly shaken, Berry made a second attempt, but to no avail. Heaving with all his might, he succeeded only in bending the lever. An artisan warder was summoned to diagnose the problem and a saw was passed around the frame of the trapdoors to relieve possible pressure on the wooden boards, swollen by overnight rain. Satisfied that the fault had now been remedied, the prisoner was recalled to face his ordeal for a third time. Berry drew the bolt but the scaffold merely shuddered and the execution was abandoned. John Lee was returned to his cell, seemingly unaffected by his torment; he then suddenly remembered an extraordinary occurrence, which he had recounted earlier that morning to two warders: 'I saw it all in a dream! I was led down to the scaffold and it would not work – after three attempts, they brought me back to my cell!'

Lee's agonising experience brought about a wave of public sympathy and indignation, typified by the response of Queen Victoria, who reacted strongly in favour of Lee even though she had been personally acquainted with the murder victim. She made her feelings known in a telegram to the Home Secretary: 'I am horrified at the disgraceful scenes at Exeter at Lee's execution. Surely Lee cannot now be executed. It would be too cruel. Imprisonment for life seems the only alternative.'

Although an official report concluded that the scaffold had failed due to a simple mechanical fault, the findings were not made public and many people believed God had acted to save an innocent man. After serving twenty-two years' imprisonment, Lee was released in December 1907 and was greeted home like a hero.

He sold his life story to a national newspaper and established a different reputation as a 'lady killer', receiving several proposals of marriage before choosing Jessie Bulled. The wedding took place in Newton Abbot in January 1909 and the couple immediately left for Newcastle, where Lee took up employment making personal appearances at a public house. Two years later he was filling a similar position in London at Ye Olde King's Head, Southwark, where he began an affair with barmaid Adelina Gibbs. He then callously abandoned his wife without support while she was expecting their second child, and emigrated with his new love to Milwaukee, USA, where he resided until his death, aged eighty, in 1945. He had survived sixty years more than was expected when he escaped death on the scaffold – a turn of events that embarrassed the editor of the *Dartmouth & Brixham Chronicle*, who rushed out an early edition prematurely announcing, 'The condemned man John Lee was executed... the culprit died easily'.

Harry Grant: The Armless Killer

Armless Harry Grant,
Launched a murderous attack.
Walked to the railway station,
And lay down on the track.

Verse by Mike Holgate.

Harry Grant was a plumber's mate serving on steam-powered naval vessels. In June 1872, his world changed dramatically whilst travelling home to spend leave with his parents (who ran a tearoom in Torquay). As the train approached his final destination, the sailor leaned out of the carriage door – which suddenly flew open, flinging him on to the line beneath the wheels of the carriage. He was taken to hospital suffering from serious injuries which necessitated the amputation of his left arm.

Invalided from the service with a small pension, the twenty-five-year-old became depressed about his future and twice attempted suicide; even the love of a woman twelve years his junior failed to quell Grant's bouts of melancholia. In 1884 he married Sarah Daymond, the daughter of a mason from Bovey Tracey. The groom was now working as a house painter while his bride was a charwoman for two elderly sisters in Newton Abbot. The couple settled in the town and Grant obtained employment at the Great Western Railway depot carrying out paint jobs. Problems surfaced during the couple's tenth anniversary when Sarah became pregnant with her first child. Grant's happiness was dispelled when he went to Newton Races, where he met an acquaintance called

Harry Grant.

Mrs Barker who suggested – in crude terms – that he was not the father because his wife had been 'going round with other men'.

Despite having absolutely no evidence of his wife's infidelity, Grant chose to believe that she had been unfaithful and refused to accept the child as his own. When the baby boy was born at their terraced home in Lemon Road in September 1894, a neighbour, Catherine Massey, acted as midwife, and then had to intercede in an ugly scene as Grant saw the baby for the first time. As Sarah cradled her child, Grant grabbed a bottle and held it threateningly over mother and baby, until Mrs Massey appeared and persuaded him to put the weapon down. Her husband's hatred of the child forced Sarah to arrange for another couple to raise the baby from the age of six months. Although the Grants no longer shared a bedroom and the marriage was effectively over, the couple continued to live together. The relationship deteriorated even further, and the couple were often heard locked in slanging matches. On one occasion Grant was heard to shout, 'I'll knock her brains out, that's what I'll do with the cow'. Why Sarah Grant chose to stay with her husband in such a hostile atmosphere is a mystery, but there was little surprise among the residents of Lemon Road at the shocking final outcome, labelled 'The Newton Tragedy'.

On Sunday, 9 August 1896, Grant left his home shortly before 8 a.m. and walked to the railway station. Suicide was his intention, and he lay on the line in front of a train leaving the station. He was spotted by the driver, who put the locomotive into reverse to slow the train; the lifeguard attached to the front of the engine pushed Grant off the track. Once again Grant had failed in his attempt to die. He suffered scalp wounds and bruising to his ribs and chest, but ironically the worst injury incurred was to his one remaining arm. The elbow joint was terribly mangled and crushed, rendering the arm useless. The patient was rushed to hospital but refused to give the surgeon permission to amputate the limb, as he 'did not care whether he lived or died'.

A railway worker, accompanied by two policemen, went to inform Mrs Grant about the incident involving her husband and discovered a grisly scene. The unfortunate woman had been attacked and left for dead in her bedroom. Despite her agonising injuries, with horrific skull fractures caused by six hammer blows to the head, Sarah Grant survived a further two days before death ended her suffering. She occasionally regained consciousness, but was unable to communicate and thereby shed any light on the incident. A policeman had observed Harry Grant staggering home drunk from the Railway Hotel on the evening of the brutal attack and neighbours had heard the couple rowing at midnight. Grant denied culpability but was charged with murder. His trial was held at Exeter Castle. Medical opinions expressed in the courtroom varied as to the state of mind of the accused, and the judge, Mr Justice Wills, summed up the quandary for the jury: 'Incidents showed the man's mind was not so strong as it might be, but did it show that when he killed his wife he did not know he was killing a human being and offending against the laws of God and man?'

The jury retired and took only a quarter of an hour to return a verdict of 'guilty, with a recommendation to mercy'. The judge assumed the black cap and passed sentence of death, commenting: 'The jury have returned the only verdict which it seems to me they, as honest men, could do. That you killed this woman in this cruel way there could be no doubt. They have accompanied the verdict with a recommendation to mercy. That will be forwarded to the Secretary of State'.

The execution was set for Wednesday 9 December and in his devout ministrations with Exeter Prison chaplain, the Reverend John Pitkin, the condemned man was said 'to view his approaching end with cheerfulness' and 'has no desire that the efforts being made to save his life shall be successful'. However, following an appeal submitted by his solicitor Frederick Carter, the Home Secretary, Sir Matthew White Ridley, granted a reprieve to the prisoner – despite the absence of any petition organised by even his family or friends. As the *East & South Devon Advertiser* observed, 'In Newton Abbot, where the prisoner was best known, the respite occasioned some surprise… The public were unusually indifferent… not the slightest move was made to save the man's life. The feeling in the town was altogether the other way'. The newspaper also commented that as the prisoner was 'probably as sane as most people at large' and not eligible to join the lunatic inmates of Broadmoor; as his disabilities rendered him incapable of the 'hard labour' duties demanded of prisoners: 'There is naturally much speculation about what will be done with the convict. If he is sent to penal servitude he will never be able to work. He will always have to be waited on and dressed and fed like a child, as it is almost certain that he will never regain the use of his arm… It is a curious case, and probably one of the most difficult the convict authorities have ever had to deal with.'

For Harry Grant, clemency was probably a greater punishment than execution; his fervent wish to die was denied and his disability rendered him incapable of ending his life by 'his own hand'.

Herbert Rowse Armstrong: The Dandelion Killer

Herbert Rowse Armstrong took a woman's life,
Administered poison and found another wife.
The Dandelion Killer planned the perfect crime,
They hanged him when he tried it one more time.

From folk song 'The Dandelion Killer' by Mike Holgate.

The Court of Appeal hears the case for Armstrong.

In 1905, the mother of John 'Babbacombe' Lee engaged the services of Newton Abbot solicitor Herbert Rowse Armstrong to try and gain his release from prison. Attempting to enlist the support of local MP Harry Eve, Armstrong wrote: 'I am quite aware that there is no statutory definition or power to diminish a life sentence, but the Home Office regulations do constantly allow of its reduction to twenty years and often less, e.g. Mrs. Maybrick,

King Edward VII lays the foundation stone at Dartmouth. Armstrong was part of his guard of honour.

as to almost nullify the effect'. The writer of the letter little realised that a quarter of a century hence, he, like the aforementioned Florence Maybrick, would deny charges of poisoning a spouse and be condemned to stand on the scaffold. The difference was that there would be no reprieve for Armstrong, and he would go down in the annals of criminal history as the only solicitor ever to be hanged for murder.

Born in 1869 at Plymouth, Herbert Rowse Armstrong gained a degree at Cambridge University. In 1901, he completed his legal training, and set up practice in Newton Abbot. Living with his mother and two maiden aunts, they all attended the local Congregational church where Armstrong was made a deacon and appointed secretary. As a lieutenant in the Devon Volunteers, he was the driving force of the Newton Abbot section of the Torquay Company of Royal Engineers. It was a proud moment for the dapper officer when he led his men to serve as a guard of honour to King Edward VII at Dartmouth where His Majesty laid the foundation stone of the Britannia Royal Naval College in 1902.

Katherine and Herbert Rowse Armstrong.

In June 1907, Armstrong married his fiancée of three years, Katherine Friend, in her home town, Teignmouth, and took up practice in the Welsh border town of Hay-on-Wye. Armstrong continued his military interest as a member of the Territorial Army, and during the First World War was called upon to serve in various locations on home soil, attaining the rank of major (which he retained upon his return to civilian life). During this period of military service he fell in love with another woman, but was faced with the obstacle of his nagging wife, Katherine. It was widely known among their friends and acquaintances that she 'henpecked' her husband. People felt sorry for the little man, who was routinely humiliated by his spouse. Famously, for example, she once turned up at his tennis club and summoned him home in the middle of a match by reminding him loudly, in front of other members, that it was his 'bath night'.

Demobbed in 1919, Armstrong found it hard to pick up his neglected business and soon ran into financial difficulties. As his law practice foundered, he was apparently more concerned about a patch of dandelions on his lawn and, despite employing the services of a jobbing gardener, bought several quantities of arsenic to treat them himself. By August 1920, Katherine Armstrong was in failing health. Her condition steadily deteriorated, and she passed away in February 1921. Her bereaved husband now turned his attention to fellow solicitor Oswald Martin, with whom he was professionally involved on opposite sides of a protracted property sale. Martin came to tea, and ate a buttered scone which was placed on a plate by his apologetic host with the words, 'Excuse fingers'. Later that night, Martin was violently ill and two months later, on New Year's Eve, 1921, the locality was shocked to learn that the major had been arrested for attempted murder. Gossip ran like wildfire through the community as the police investigation switched to the churchyard, where the body of Katherine Armstrong was exhumed. Medical examination found evidence to suggest that she had been poisoned.

Motives for his wife's murder were soon made evident – money and another woman. The victim's sister, Ida Bessie Friend, travelled from her home in Torquay, and testified that Katherine had made a will in 1917 which had been witnessed by herself and another Torquay lady, Augusta Gertrude Hutchins, who was then acting as nurse-companion to the deceased. The £2,500 estate was divided into a small bequest for her long-serving housekeeper, with the remainder to be put into trust for the three children, while her husband was not left anything. It emerged that during Katherine's illness Armstrong forged his wife's signature on a new will naming him as sole beneficiary. Addressing the subject of the major's love life, the court was stunned to learn from a physician that the major had consorted with prostitutes and contracted a sexually transmitted disease. Furthermore, within three months of his wife's death he had proposed marriage to a fifty-year-old widow, Marion Gale, whom he had met during the war years.

The 'Hay Poisoner' was apprehended when Oscar Martin was taken seriously ill in October after eating the buttered scone handed to him by Armstrong. Dr Hincks was called to treat the ailing solicitor and sent off a sample of his urine to a clinic for analysis. The result showed that it contained a substantial amount of arsenic. The truth suddenly began to dawn as chemist John Davies, who was Martin's father-in-law, revealed he had supplied Armstrong with quantities of the deadly chemical. Dr Hinks also realised that his patient, Katherine Armstrong, had suffered from similar symptoms. Their suspicions were referred for investigation to the police, who finally acted when Martin became terrified by another barrage of invitations to dine with Armstrong. The major had been stalling on a property deal, in which he had a considerable financial stake, for over eighteen months, and the purchasers represented by Martin withdrew their offer. Even with his wife's inheritance, Armstrong was unable to refund a £500 deposit demanded by Martin's clients and was sliding towards insolvency.

Major Armstrong's old friends in Newton Abbot greeted the outcome of the trial with incredulity; likewise, many people in Hay-on-Wye agreed that the mild-mannered major was incapable of such wicked acts. If he had committed murder, it seemed extraordinary to his supporters that the accused would not eliminate all prospect of any suspicion arising against him in the future by simply arranging for the body of his wife to be cremated. The defence counsel contended that Katherine Armstrong's mental state caused her to commit suicide, but this notion was dismissed by the trial judge: he reminded the jury of the victim's final words to her nurse, 'I'm not going to die, am I? I have so much to live for; my husband and my children'.

Writer Edgar Wallace, who covered executions for the *Daily Mail,* offered the then considerable sum of £5,000 to the condemned man to acknowledge his guilt, but although that money could have helped to secure the future for his three soon-to-be-orphaned children, Armstrong refused the opportunity to make an exclusive 'confession' and was hanged at Gloucester Prison in May 1922, denying his guilt to the end: 'I am innocent of the crime for which I have been condemned to die.'

Robert Hichens: The Sinking of the *Titanic* Helmsman

Bob Hichens was at the wheel when the ship began to keel,
Fare thee well *Titanic,* fare thee well,
She sank beneath the waves taking people to their graves,
Fare thee well, *Titanic,* fare thee well.

Adapted from song 'Fare thee well, *Titanic*' by Huddie Ledbetter.

The sinking of the *Titanic*.

Robert Hichens was the helmsman at the wheel of the *Titanic* when the much vaunted 'unsinkable' vessel struck an iceberg and sank, with the loss of 1,500 lives, in 1912. Put in charge of a lifeboat, Hichens was criticised at the subsequent inquiry, held in a New York hotel owned by Plymouth MP Waldorf Astor, for swigging whiskey and ignoring pleas from other occupants of the boat to search the water for survivors. 'No,' he said curtly, 'we are not going back to the boat. It is our lives now, not theirs.' As the ship disappeared beneath the waves, the cries and screams of people fighting for their lives in the water were plainly heard in the still night air. Hichens cruelly summed up the situation: 'It's no use; there's only a lot of stiffs out there.'

The inhumane attitude and over-reliance on drink displayed by Hichens at this great moment of crisis was to re-surface some twenty years later in Torquay, where he failed to make a living running pleasure boat trips. It was in the same town, during the summer of 1906, that he had met his future wife, Florence Mortimore. She was visiting relatives in the resort, while he was on shore leave with the crew of a private yacht. Following a whirlwind courtship, the couple were married within a few months at the parish church in the bride's home village of Manaton on Dartmoor. Settling first in Torquay, where their first two of six children were born, then Southampton, Hichens secured a prestigious appointment on the newly launched luxury liner *Titanic*. Following the terrible maritime disaster, he returned to sea, served with the naval reserve during the First World War, and then spent some time working with one of his brothers in South Africa. By 1930, he was back in Torquay as owner of the *Princess Elizabeth* pleasure boat, purchased from businessman Harry Henley for the sum of £160 (of which he paid a down payment of £100, with the remainder to be paid within two years). The venture failed disastrously and he was unable to repay the balance. Furthermore, Hichens had borrowed the deposit from a Mr Squires, who seized the boat to settle the debt following a poor season's trading in 1931. The loss of his business caused Hichens to turn to drink, and by the end of that year his wife had left him and moved back to Southampton.

For the next two years her troubled husband scoured the country, unable to find work. Unreasonably, he chose to lay the blame for his predicament on the man who had sold him the boat. On his travels he had acquired a revolver for £5, and on 12 November 1933 he journeyed to Torquay, determined to kill Harry Henley upon his arrival. He looked up an old friend of twenty years' standing, fisherman Thomas Holden, and told him, 'There will be two less in Torquay tonight. I've come down to do Henley and myself.' By early evening Hichens was drinking with another acquaintance, docker Joe Stroud, who hearing of the plan, and shown the revolver, warned, 'Put it away. Don't be a fool. He isn't worth swinging for.'

Robert Hichens giving evidence at the *Titanic* inquiry.

Worse the wear for drink, the gunman appeared to see sense and replied, 'I'll take your tip. I shan't give the hangman a job'. Later, while walking near the harbour with Stroud, he saw Henley as the pair passed each other without exchanging a word. However, after closing time, having consumed rum in at least three public houses during the course of the evening, Hichens took a taxi, driven by Harry Scrivings, who dropped him off outside Harry Henley's house at Stentiford's Hill, Torquay.

Hearing a knock at the door, Henley came outside to see Hichens standing with both hands in his trouser pockets. 'Do you remember me, Harry?' slurred the inebriated Hichens. 'Why, of course I do!' replied Henley. 'What do you want?' The unexpected caller asked him for money, saying 'I am on the ground. I want you to pick me up.' Henley naturally replied, 'Why do you expect me to pick you up when you owe me £60 already?' Hichens became apologetic: 'I am sorry. It is all through the drink that I am like this.' Referring to the debt, the out-of-pocket Henley, who had made no attempt to recover the money owed to him, commented, 'I have to suffer for that as well as you. I won't lend you a penny because you have been a rogue and a scamp to me.' Hichens gripped the revolver in his right-hand pocket and demanded, 'Is that your last word?' To which his creditor replied,

'I wouldn't give you a penny piece if you were lying in the gutter.'
Hichens then pulled out the pistol and with the words 'Take that'
raised the weapon to the level of his target's head. In the dimly
lit porch, Henley thought that Hichens was going to strike him
with his fist and instinctively put up his arm to ward off a blow.
Two gunshot explosions followed as Hichens fired the revolver
at point-blank range and very nearly succeeded in his desire to
kill his former business associate. The first bullet grazed the side
of the victim's head. Henley felt a searing pain. He subsequently
lost a lot of blood, but was fortunate not to suffer serious injury.
The second shot went downwards and wide as Henley pushed
Hichens away and punched his assailant in the face, giving him a
bloody nose. Hichens fell to floor, giving Henley the opportunity
to run away and summon the police. Meanwhile, the gunman
got up and staggered thirty yards before laying down on the
footpath, where he tentatively put the revolver to his head and
pulled the trigger. His luck was again against him: the bullet
passed harmlessly by. Taken to the police station in an intoxicated
state, Hichens enquired, 'Is he dead? I hope he is. He is a dirty rat,
I would do it again if I had a chance. I intended to kill him and
myself, too. He has taken my living away.'

Brought to trial for attempted murder, the prisoner received a
sympathetic hearing after appearing with dressings on his wrists:
he had made a desperate attempt to slash his wrists while held in
custody. The defendant's previous good character and the fact that
he appeared to be a 'broken man' influenced the lenient outcome
of five years' imprisonment. Despite the murderous attack having
been fermenting in his mind for many months, his defence
counsel contended that the incident had been precipitated only
because his client was under the influence of alcohol. With an
unintended pun, he explained that since the terrible ordeal on the
Titanic his client had been 'sinking lower and lower'.

Chapter Two

Smugglers and Pirates

Tales of crime at sea featuring the exploits of smuggler Jack Rattenbury,
privateer Sir Francis Drake, pirate Sir Thomas Stucley and buccaneer
Henry 'Long Ben' Avery.

Sir Thomas Stucley: Defamed Throughout Christendom

Taverns and ordinaries – where his chiefest braveries,
Golden angels there flew up and down;
Riots were his best delights – with stately feasting day and night,
In court and city thus he won renown.

From a contemporary ballad about Thomas Stucley.

'If Devonshire has turned out a number, and a very considerable number of, gallant and honourable gentlemen, she has also given birth to some great scoundrels, and one of these was Thomas Stucley or Stukeley,' wrote local author, folklorist and historian the Reverend Sabine Baring-Gould in 1908. Born at Affeton Castle, near Witherbridge, in 1525, ostensibly the third son of Sir Hugh Stucley, although it was widely rumoured that he was an illegitimate child of King Henry VIII, Thomas Stucley was to match the notoriety of his later kinsman, Lewis 'Judas' Stucley, the reviled traitor who died a friendless recluse on Lundy Island after betraying and arranging the arrest and subsequent execution of national hero Sir Walter Raleigh.

Thomas 'Lusty' Stucley followed the shameful exploits of infamous pirate, mercenary and traitor after earning a reputation as a brave soldier and brilliant commander. If he was of royal blood, it might explain why the courtier then won favour with his possible step-sister Queen Elizabeth, whose influence saved him from execution for piracy after she had granted her personal support to establish a colony in Florida. Fitting out six ships for the venture in 1563, Captain Stucley got distracted and abandoned his mission to prey on treasure-laden vessels from Spain and merchantmen from France and Portugal. After filling his coffers on the high seas for two years, the protests from the governments of these countries reached such a crescendo that the deeply embarrassed queen ordered his arrest. Apprehended off the coast of Cork, Stucley was held in the Tower of London, then, despite additional reports of robbery, murder and other outrages allegedly committed by him, the charges were quietly

King Henry VIII.

Sir Thomas Stucley.

dropped through lack of evidence and he was released without punishment when the clamour for his head had calmed down.

Stucley had secretly married a rich heiress against her father's wishes and quickly squandered her fortune. In 1555, he was arrested by the Sheriff of Devon on charges of coining false money, but insufficient incriminating evidence was found and he was released. Following the death of his wife in 1564, Stucley married a rich Irish widow and took up the cause of the outlawed Catholics and their opposition to enforced Protestantism. This course of action flouted the authority of the sovereign, Queen Elizabeth, who had spared his life and was the Supreme Governor of the Church of England. Forming an alliance with England's arch enemy Spain, Stucley was created Marquis of Ireland by King Philip II and proposed an invasion of his country (which he hoped to rule). However, the king did not altogether trust Stucley and repeatedly postponed the venture, afraid his navy might be led into a trap by a double agent, despite the turncoat proving his commitment to a foreign crown by serving with distinction alongside the Spanish fleet in the victorious Battle of Lepanto against the Turks in 1571. Queen Elizabeth also doubted Stucley's loyalty and he was committed to prison, charged with using coarse language against the sovereign and supporting Irish rebels. Held in Dublin Castle, Stucley's plausible tongue gained his release eighteen weeks later after protesting his innocence and falsely swearing his unswerving loyalty to the queen.

Unable to obtain King Phillip's blessing for his enterprise in the Emerald Isle, Stucley called upon Pope Pious V for aid and was provided with a ship, 600 men and a consecrated banner to plant in Ireland. Sailing from Italy in 1578, the leaky vessel became un-seaworthy and was forced to put into Lisbon for repairs. Stucley sought the assistance of King Sebastian of Portugal, but was induced to join an attack on Morocco. Upon reaching North Africa, Stucley wisely advised the king to allow the soldiers onboard the 500 ships to recover from their long voyage, but the impulsive young sovereign immediately ordered his men to launch the disastrous Battle of Alcazar. The Portuguese invaders were overwhelmed by the vastly superior cavalry of the Moors led by Sultan Abdul-el-Malek. According to one account, Stucley fought bravely until losing both legs to a cannon shot, a wound from which he eventually perished, while another report claims that he was captured along with King Sebastian. The leaders were then triumphantly taken ashore and beheaded.

Thus perished a man who had been vilified during his lifetime by Queen Elizabeth's chief minister, William Cecil: 'Thomas Stucley, a defamed person almost through all Christendom, and a faithless beast rather than a man, fleeing first out of England for notable piracies, and out of Ireland for treacheries unpardonable.'

Sir Francis Drake: Scourge of the Spanish Main

Drake he was a Devon man, an' ruled the Devon seas,
(Capten, art tha sleepin' there below?),
Rovin' tho' his death fell, he went wi' heart at ease,
An' dreamin' arl the time o' Plymouth Hoe,
'Take my drum to England, hang et by the shore,
Strike et when your powder's runnin' low;
If the Dons sight Devon, I'll quit the port o' Heaven,
An' drum them up the Channel as we drummed them long ago.'

From poem *Drake's Drum* by Henry Newbolt.

Sir Francis Drake.

The *Golden Hind*.

Devon's most famous son, and a national hero who became a legend in his own lifetime, Sir Francis Drake's triumphs included circumnavigating the globe in 1580; 'singeing the King of Spain's beard' during a daring raid which destroyed thirty vessels in the port of Cadiz in 1587, and, a year later, playing a vital role in defeating the might of the Spanish Armada after coolly completing a game of bowls on Plymouth Hoe. His final mission proved something of an anticlimax to his glittering career. With a distinguished relative, Sir John Hawkins, they tried to recapture the glory days of their youth by launching a disastrous campaign on the Spanish Maine – where the old seadogs both succumbed to illness. They were buried at sea in 1596.

Born of humble origins at Crowndale Farm, near Tavistock, Drake's rise to prominence was built on villainy. He went to sea and learnt the art of piracy, sailing with his cousin, John Hawkins. Believing that they were justified in robbing England's Catholic enemies, the 'privateers' were eventually supported by Queen Elizabeth who granted licenses to her pirates in return for a share of the booty taken from treasure ships. Years later, when Drake circled the earth and returned to Plymouth laden with enough gold and silver to pay off the national debt, there were calls for his execution from the Spanish ambassador. However, the owners of the sacked galleons had not registered their treasure in order to avoid a Spanish levy on the shipments, and therefore, proof of theft could not be established. Drake was rewarded for his enterprise when the queen conferred a knighthood on him aboard his ship, the *Golden Hind*. Further honours were heaped on Drake when he became Lord Mayor of Plymouth and a Member of Parliament for the county. In keeping with his new-found status, he purchased a mansion on Dartmoor, the former monastery, Buckland Abbey.

The former pirate was now a gentleman, but at the height of the battle against the Spanish Armada, he returned to type and infuriated his fellow commanders by neglecting his duties to claim a rich prize. The English fleet was divided into four squadrons, commanded by the Lord Admiral, Charles Howard of Effingham, Yorkshireman Martin Frobisher, John Hawkins, and Francis Drake. The invaders were scattered to the four winds by eight fire ships sent into their midst. In the confusion that followed, the flagship *Nuestra Senora Del Rosario* collided with another galleon and was disabled, losing her foresails and bowsprit. Lord Howard's *Ark Royal* poured a broadside into the stricken vessel before seeking a more worthy prey. Then Hawkins in the *Victory* and Frobisher in the *Triumph* engaged the crippled ship before sailing away in obedience to a signal from the English flagship. Drake's ship *Revenge* was also ordered to pursue the Spanish fleet, keeping his stern lantern lit all night as a beacon for the other ships; instead, however, he extinguished the light and set off to capture the *Rosario*. The tempting prize was a pay ship carrying a fortune in wages for the soldiers of the invading army. The captain of the enemy vessel meekly surrendered his sword without a fight after receiving an ultimatum from the feared El Draco: 'I am Francis Drake and my matches are burning'. The plunder was loaded onto the *Revenge*, along with important prisoners whom Drake intended to hold for ransom. The stricken ship was then sent to Tor Bay, where 400 prisoners were taken ashore and held in an improvised prison – still remembered as 'the Spanish Barn' – on the lord of the manor's estate, Torre Abbey, at Torquay. A general order that all captives should be executed was fortunately rescinded, although the Sheriff of Devon thought it a pity to spare their lives, saying that they ought to have 'been made water spaniels'.

Drake's prize, the *Rosario*, in Tor Bay.

Hawkins and Frobisher, both knighted for their heroism in the historic sea battle, were disgusted by Drake's actions and claimed that they were entitled to a portion of the spoils. Accusing Drake of being 'a cowardly knave or a traitor' for withdrawing from the fight to line his own pockets, Frobisher threatened to kill him: 'He thinketh to cozen us of our share of the 15,000 ducats, but we will have our share, or I will make him spend the best blood in his belly, for he hath done enough of these cozening tricks already.' When questioned about the plunder, Drake defended his selfish desertion by pleading poverty. Despite having married wealthy heiress Elizabeth Sydenham three years earlier, the realm's most successful pirate, who had acquired vast amounts of treasure from over a decade of piracy, claimed he had acted out of necessity, for he had 'not three pounds left in the world'.

Long Ben: King of the Pirates

'Ho!' cried Ben and ran the grinning skull atop the mast,
'I'll wager half my share me lads, there's not a ship this fast!'
We turned the *Fancy* from the wind and ran out 40 guns,
And soon the sky was filled with smoke that hid us from the sun.

Then up and down the ship we fought, until the decks ran red,
And when the fight was done we drank and this is what we said:
Here's to gentlemen at sea tonight and a toast to all free men,
And when the Devil comes to take us home,
We'll drink to old Long Ben!

From contemporary broadsheet, *The Ballad of Long Ben.*

Budding pirate Henry Avery was born at Newton Ferrers near Plymouth in 1659. The sea was in his blood, for his father had served under Admiral Blake but died whilst his son was quite young. Henceforth, Henry would be known by his father's name, John. The child's widowed mother kept a tavern and her youngster got his first taste of life at sea when she refused to serve a party of drunken sailors – who then carried off the landlady's son in revenge. The lad was press-ganged into taking a voyage for three years before returning home, having been treated well by the ship's captain during his sojourn at sea.

Obviously undaunted by his enforced experience at sea, Avery joined the Royal Navy and served for many years as a midshipman before joining a privateering expedition as first mate on the *Charles II*, one of four armed merchant ships that sailed from Plymouth to salvage treasure ships in the Caribbean in 1693. Once under sail, Avery incited the crew to mutiny; morale was low, as their pay was long overdue. Reasoning that 'I am a man of fortune, therefore I must seek my fortune', Avery transformed himself at the age of thirty-four into the infamous buccaneer 'Long Ben'.

Avery announced he was seizing the ship by waking the captain from his drunken slumber and declaring, 'Don't be alarmed, put on your clothes and I'll let you into a secret. You must know that now I am captain of the ship, and that henceforth this is my cabin, so please to walk out of it. I am bound for Madagascar to seek my fortune and that of the brave fellows who have joined with me.'

The captain and his supporters among the crew were then put into a longboat. Renaming the ship *Fancy*, Avery carried out his plan by heading for the pirate stronghold of Madagascar. Along the way, he looted several treasure ships and tricked natives into believing they were traders. As soon as the boats approached

'Long Ben' and his ship, the *Fancy*.

Captain Avery accompanied by a slave.

bearing gold, the unsuspecting occupants were robbed, clapped in irons and later sold as slaves for a handsome profit. Roaming the Indian Ocean, Avery caused an international incident by leading an attack on a ship conveying pilgrims to Mecca. The vessel was owned by the Indian Emperor of the Moguls and Avery kidnapped one of the passengers, the Emperor's daughter, who was held for ransom. A warrant for the arrest of Avery was issued when 'The Great Mogul' threatened to suspend trade with England. Now a fugitive with a price on his head, 'Long Ben' dumped the girl on Madagascar, changed his vessel in an effort to avoid detection and steered a course for Nassau (where he hoped to obtain a pardon). However, when he arrived at his destination he discovered his presence was unwelcome. Six of his crew who had parted company with the pirate ship were subsequently caught and tried at the Old Bailey in London, and five of them were hanged in 1696.

Having sailed up the American coast with a crew of eighteen Irishmen unsuccessfully seeking a safe haven, Avery turned his vessel and sailed to Cork, where all except 'Long Ben' received pardons from the newly crowned king, William III.

What became of Avery after this date has never been substantiated, although it was rumoured that he fled from Ireland

and returned to his native county, landing at Bideford in North Devon. Assuming a new identity, he hoped to live down his reputation as 'King of the Pirates' by settling for the quiet life with his ill-gotten gains. Wanting to cash in his valuable assets, he approached a firm of Bristol merchants with a bag of diamonds that were part of the booty stolen from the Emperor's ship. Realising the true identity of the rogue they were dealing with, the merchants kept the jewels and palmed the seller off with a derisory amount of money under threat of exposure to the legal authorities, who were anxious to apprehend and execute their quarry. According to this tale, Avery remained in Bideford a broken man, soon fell ill and died a beggar, having never recovered from the ignominy of being cheated out of a fortune won on the high seas by a band of corrupt 'land lubbers'.

Jack Rattenbury: Rob Roy of the West

Rob Roy of the West,
Tried to outwit the law,
Smuggling contraband ashore,
Resisting arrest,
Rob Roy of the West.

From folk song 'Rob Roy of the West' by Mike Holgate.

Jack Rattenbury recorded his adventures in an autobiography published before his death cataloguing over a dozen thrilling escapes from the hands of the press gang who attempted to force him into the navy, or the preventative men who were always trying to apprehend the rogue during his many years of smuggling activities. This illicit trade earned him the title 'Rob Roy of the West'.

Born at East Devon in the village of Beer in 1778, the son of a local shoemaker who was press-ganged and never seen again by his family, young Jack was apprenticed to a Brixham trawlerman before running away a year later complaining that he had been ill-treated by his employer. Constantly pursued by press gangs, he

Jack Rattenbury.

got his first real experience of life at sea at the age of fourteen, when he willingly joined the crew of a privateer licensed to attack enemy shipping. This venture was also to give him his first taste of prison life, for he was captured by the French and thrown into a Bordeaux prison for some time before gaining his release. In 1800 he was captured again, this time by the Spanish, and imprisoned at Vigo, but continued to pursue a life of adventure and undeserved wealth until the age of twenty-seven, later recalling that roaming the seas had made him feel 'like a bird which had escaped from a cage'.

Finally abandoning his career as a privateer, Jack married Anna Partridge in 1801 and worked as a pilot, guiding ships to safety for four years; he then took up fishing in Beer, where he was drawn into making regular smuggling jaunts to the Channel Islands and France. Inevitably, he was eventually caught and taken to Dartmouth Castle, where he was given the option of imprisonment or naval service. After spending an uncomfortable night in the cells, he chose the latter and was taken onboard a waiting man-o-war. Ever the man of action, he immediately seized an opportunity to escape by jumping overboard. Swimming to a

Dartmouth Castle.

small boat nearby, the deserter paid the owner to drop him off on the opposite shore at Kingswear. Making his way to Brixham, Jack completed his escape by taking a fishing smack home to Beer.

Resuming his smuggling expeditions, Jack was apprehended again when returning with contraband from Alderney. Taken to Falmouth in Cornwall, he was sentenced to imprisonment in Bodmin Gaol, but planned an escape when the constables escorting him stopped off at every public house *en route*. When the policemen returned to the coach after making merry at a tavern in Indian Queens, a scuffle broke out and their prisoner made a bolt for freedom. As the fugitive ran away, a ball fired from a pistol by one of the inebriated constables narrowly missed his head. Making good his escape, Jack hired a horse and made his way to Newquay, before completing his journey home by boat to Devon. Public houses were the scene of further escapades when Jack once avoided arrest by hiding up the chimney whist the premises were being searched for his presence and, on another occasion, by jumping into a cellar and holding off the guardians of the law for four hours before they were distracted by some local women who urged them to leave to help a boy who they falsely claimed was in danger of drowning. His wife twice impeded would-be captors trying to either impress or imprison her husband.

Other of his numerous brushes with the law whist carrying out shady dealings included spells of imprisonment at Exeter and Dorchester. He was also fortunate not to receive further punishment, having been caught transporting four enemy prisoners of war who had escaped from custody at Tiverton during the Napoleonic Wars.

However, despite Jack Rattenbury's tales of hair's-breadth escapes, brief imprisonments, successful free-booting expeditions and his jocular boast that he 'cut up preventative men for crab bait', it appears the renowned smuggler made little profit from his lawless career. Retiring from his chosen trade at the age of fifty-eight, having been forced to abandon his last cargo of contraband when challenged by customs officials during a run from Torquay, severe gout and reduced circumstances compelled him to accept a small pension, paid until his death aged sixty-five in 1844, by one of the former recipients of his imported goods, Lord Rolle. Looking back on his life, the scoundrel explained why he had abandoned fishing for smuggling: 'I found the employment very dull and tiresome after the roving life I had led; and as the smuggling trade was then plied very briskly in the neighbourhood. I determined to try my fortune in it.'

Chapter Three

Traitors

Hanging was considered suitable only for low-life criminals; therefore, the axe man was employed to behead the following aristocrats who earned the sovereign's wrath: Lord Edward Seymour, Lady Jane Grey, Sir Walter Raleigh and the Duke of Monmouth.

Lord Edward Seymour: Protector of the Realm

Queen Jane was in labour for six days or more,
And the midwives were weary and wished it was o'er.
She wept and she wailed till she fell in a swoon,
So they opened her sides and Prince Edward was born.
The baby was christened with joy and much mirth,
Whilst poor Queen Jane's body lay cold in the earth.
There was ringing and singing and mourning all day,
King Henry was weeping with joy and dismay.

Adapted from traditional ballad 'The Death of Queen Jane'.

Lord Edward Seymour had recently been appointed Protector of the Realm, with full authority to conduct affairs of state on behalf of his youthful nephew, King Edward VI, when he acquired the town of Totnes and the nearby village of Berry Pomeroy in 1547. The previous owner, staunch Roman Catholic Sir Thomas Pomeroy, was arrested two years later for his role in the Western Rebellion. In an act of treason, he helped to raise an army of 10,000 Devonians and led them into battle in protest against church reforms introduced by the Calvinist Protector. Nevertheless, Seymour treated Pomeroy mercifully and ordered his release; four of his fellow conspirators paid the full penalty for their actions, and were hung, drawn and quartered.

Thomas Pomeroy was indeed fortunate, for the Lord Protector acted ruthlessly when his authority was challenged by his own brother, Thomas Seymour. The warring siblings' influence in royal circles had come about through the marriage of their sister Jane Seymour, who became the third wife of King Henry VIII. A former lady-in-waiting to Catherine of Aragon and Anne Boleyn, Jane succeeded where her predecessors had failed in satisfying the monarch's obsession with providing a male heir but died in the process of delivering their son, Edward. To marry Jane, Henry broke away from Rome, founded the Church of England, then had his marriage to Anne Boleyn annulled before ordering her execution on charges of adultery and incest with her brother.

Above: Berry Pomeroy, owned by Thomas Seymour.

Left: Jane Seymour.

Following the death of 'Bluff King Hal' in 1547, Thomas Seymour, Lord Admiral of England, had a proposal of marriage rejected by the advisors of Princess Elizabeth, Henry's thirteen-year-old daughter by the ill-fated Anne Boleyn, then outraged his brother by marrying Catherine Parr, the sixth wife and widow of Henry VIII, whilst the country was still in mourning for the monarch.

When Catherine died in childbirth a year later, Thomas wasted no time in trying to strengthen his standing at court by renewing his attempts to obtain the hand of Elizabeth (who remained unmarried and was dubbed the 'Virgin Queen'). Thomas also tried to usurp his brother by trying to arrange a marriage between his ward, Jane Grey, and King Edward when the children were barely ten years old. The Protector had similar plans for his own daughter and the young king, and resented this obvious threat to his royal authority. Despite pleading with Thomas to abandon his intrigues and ambitions, Edward could not dissuade his brother from further involvement in a plot to oust him from office. This latest affront could not be overlooked and Edward had no hesitation in sanctioning the trial and resultant execution of his unrepentant brother in 1549.

However, even this drastic course action did not protect Seymour from his enemies for long. Soon after quelling the Western Rebellion, he was toppled from power by John Dudley, the Duke of Northumberland. He pleaded guilty to numerous charges of profiting from the Dissolution of Monasteries and sale of church lands and received a full pardon. Despite an uneasy alliance forged by the marriage of Seymour's daughter to Northumberland's son in 1551, Seymour was arrested six months later for allegedly plotting to murder his archrival, Dudley. The prisoner was conveyed along the River Thames from the Tower to Westminster and tried by his peers. He was acquitted of treason but condemned to death for felony – charges relating to Seymour's debts to the young king. Seymour still enjoyed popular support and a contemporary source reported that after the trial the people 'made such a shriek and casting up of caps, that it was heard into the Long Acre beyond Charing Cross' and all along the route back to the Tower there were cries of 'God Save Him'.

Because of the widely-held sympathy for Seymour, an order was given for the public to stay away from the place of execution at Tower Hill, but this was ignored and a huge crowd gathered to witness the event. With great dignity, Seymour pronounced his loyalty to the king, and then calmly laid his head on the block. As the executioner's axe fell, his supporters surged forward to dip their handkerchiefs in his blood. Seymour was buried in the

Tower of London between Anne Boleyn and Catherine Howard, the two unfortunate wives of Henry VIII who had also suffered the unkindest cut!

Lady Jane Grey: The Nine Days Queen

In England the briefest reign,
That was ever seen,
Was served by Jane Grey,
The Nine Days Queen.

Verse by Mike Holgate.

Henry VIII's six marriages produced three monarchs. Undesired daughters, who earned his displeasure and the disposal of their mothers, produced two queens – Mary I and Elizabeth I. Despite both princesses being branded illegitimate by their father, they were each to be handed an opportunity in the wake of a sole male heir – the sickly Edward VI, who succeeded to the throne in 1547 at the age of nine. Six years later, as he lay dying of consumption, he was persuaded by his chief advisers to pass over the claims of his half-sisters and

four other possible claimants to the throne and nominate his first cousin as the next in line. Sixteen-year-old Lady Jane Grey swooned when told that Edward had passed away and she had been proclaimed monarch. However, her reign was to be briefest in England's history, and she is forever remembered as the 'Nine Days Queen'.

Granddaughter of Henry VIII's younger sister Mary, Lady Jane became an unwitting political pawn in a dynastic power game.

Lady Jane Grey.

Raised at Boringdon Hall, Colebrook, Plympton, she spent a happy and contented childhood at the family home until her destiny was sealed when she was compelled to leave Devon. When barely nine, she entered the household of Henry's widow, Catherine Parr, and was chief mourner when her mistress died two years later in 1548. Catherine's second husband, Lord Admiral of England, Thomas Seymour, then purchased the wardship of Jane from her parents, a distasteful but common practice which gave him the right to administer Jane's estate, also enabling him to profit politically and financially by determining whom she would marry. Seymour planned to use his influence to arrange a betrothal between Jane and Edward VI. However, his brother, Edward Seymour, owner of Totnes and Berry Pomeroy Castle, was zealously planning a union between the young king and his own daughter, whilst hoping to marry off Jane to his eldest son. The scheming brothers' plans to gain control of the kingdom resulted from the fact that their sister, Jane Seymour, had died giving birth to Edward VI. Edward Seymour took advantage of this family connection to become the power behind the throne as Lord Protector – effectively ruling the country on behalf of his royal brother-in-law. He dealt with the threat from the palace intrigues of Thomas by reluctantly authorising his headstrong brother's execution. However, Edward had made many other enemies in court circles, which cost him his own life when he was also beheaded on trumped-up charges of treason.

Following the fall of the Seymours, Lady Jane's father, the Duke of Suffolk, then allied himself with the ambitious John Dudley, Duke of Northumberland – a powerful member of the Privy Council who had overthrown and succeeded Edward Seymour. Northumberland obtained the king's sanction for his son Guildford Dudley to marry Jane in 1553. The match was made against her will and she only went through with the ceremony after she was threatened with violence by her father. The stress she suffered quickly brought on a serious illness that almost proved fatal. This union was a plot to alter the succession from the Tudors to the Dudleys, which Edward VI readily accepted because he felt closer to Jane than to his half-sisters Mary and Elizabeth. The rightful heir was Mary, Henry VIII's eldest daughter by Catherine of Aragon, who evaded a kidnap attempt by Northumberland before her supporters mounted a successful armed rising. Jane and her husband were arrested and consigned to the Tower of London. Pleading guilty to high treason, they were sentenced to death. Queen Mary was disposed to extend mercy until Jane's father foolishly participated in a revolt of Kent peasants led by Sir Thomas Wyatt following the announcement that Mary would marry the Roman Catholic, Philip of Spain. Any further Protestant insurgence was discouraged by 'Bloody Mary', who snuffed out any remaining threat from subjects loyal to Jane. Sixty people were executed, including Jane's father and father-in-law. Resigned to her fate, Jane refused to see her husband on the morning of their execution, lest the meeting disturb 'the holy tranquillity with which they had prepared themselves for death'. However, when escorted to the scaffold she was cruelly exposed to the bleeding, headless body of her luckless spouse before she too knelt beneath the shadow of the executioner's axe. From the scaffold, she made a speech asserting that she had never desired the crown and that she was to die 'a true Christian woman'.

Sir Walter Raleigh: Betrayed by 'Judas' Stucley

Sir Walter Raleigh won favour by laying,
A cloak at the feet of Queen Bess.
But he lost his head in a quarrel,
And subsequently the headman's axe.

Verse by Mike Holgate.

Brilliant courtier, parliamentarian, businessman, soldier, seaman, coloniser, explorer, scientist, philosopher, historian and poet, Walter Raleigh was one of the most celebrated men of the Elizabethan age before he became embroiled in political intrigue which brought about his execution – intrigue aided and abetted by his traitorous distant cousin Lord Lewis Stucley, who became a figure of hatred at court where he was branded 'the Judas of Devonshire'.

Born at Hayes Barton, East Budleigh, Raleigh tried to emulate his illustrious half-brother Sir Humphrey Gilbert, 'The Father of

HAYES BARTON
near EXMOUTH
Birthplace of Sir Walter Raleigh
BORN 1552, DIED 1618

Colonisation', by organising attempts to set up English colonies in North America. He won favour with Queen Elizabeth by naming Virginia in honour of the monarch known as the 'Virgin Queen'. In return, 'Good Queen Bess' bestowed a knighthood on Raleigh and enabled him to become one of the richest men in England when she granted him lucrative monopolies in the wine and cloth trades. Administrative posts were obtained in Devon, where he was appointed Vice-Admiral, Warden of the Stannaries, and also represented the county in the House of Commons. In 1592, Raleigh upset the queen by secretly marrying one of her maids of honour without seeking the sovereign's permission and he was briefly locked up in the Tower of London. Three years later he tried to restore his fortunes by leading an expedition to South America to find the fabled golden city of El Dorado. Returning empty-handed failed to impress the queen, and he was wrongly accused by some critics of never even making the voyage.

The death of Queen Elizabeth in 1603 brought about an even greater change in Raleigh's fortunes. His enemies at court spread rumours that he was opposed to the accession of King James. The new monarch immediately ordered his arrest and Raleigh was tried for treason, declared guilty and sentenced to death. On the eve of the execution he was granted a reprieve and committed to the Tower of London. Here, he was allowed special privileges – living in relative comfort accompanied by his wife, son and personal servants – but was held for thirteen years. During his captivity, he conducted scientific experiments and undertook a daunting literary work, *The History of the World*.

Sir Walter Raleigh.

In 1616, Raleigh was released and given another opportunity to redeem his reputation by undertaking an expedition to Guiana to search for gold. He was now over sixty and fell ill in Trinidad, which he had claimed for the crown twenty years earlier. The rest of the party carried on without him, but suffered many losses when they landed on Spanish territory and were apprehended by a patrol. Raleigh's son Wat was killed and the second-in-command of the venture was so ashamed of the failure that he stabbed himself in the heart. The expedition returned to Plymouth in disgrace and with the Spanish ambassador demanding that Raleigh should die; the Vice Admiral of Devonshire, Lord Lewis Stucley of Affeton Castle, near Witherbridge, was offered a reward by King James to elicit some damning evidence against Raleigh by accompanying him on his journey to London. Meeting his kinsman twenty miles from Plymouth at Ashburton, Stucley pretended to sympathise with Raleigh's plight and offered to help him flee to France on a vessel moored at Tilbury Docks. However, the party was suddenly surrounded by armed guards and at a prearranged signal Stucley revealed his true colours by proclaiming, 'Sir Walter Raleigh, I arrest you in the King's name. Gentlemen, your prisoner. Guard him well, for he is a desperate man who has just tried to escape.'

Raleigh was held prisoner in the Tower once more, while the king appointed a commission to assess the charges arising out of the Guiana fiasco and the incriminating reports of his behaviour since his return to England. They decided that as the prisoner had never been granted a pardon, the only legal grounds for execution

The execution of Raleigh.

were to enforce the death sentence passed in 1603. Raleigh poured out his despair in a letter to his wife, comparing his dilemma with that faced by two of Devon's most famous seafarers: 'As Sir Francis Drake and Sir John Hawkins died broken-hearted when they failed of their enterprise, I would willingly do the like, did I not contend against sorrow, in hope to provide somewhat for you in comfort.'

'Judas' Stucley died a recluse on Lundy.

Brushing aside thoughts of suicide, he resolved 'to die in the light not in the darkness'. On the scaffold, Raleigh's final impassioned speech lasted for forty-five minutes. He refuted all the charges against him, yet graciously forgave Stucley. Raleigh declined the offer of a blindfold from the headsman: 'Think you I fear the shadow of the axe, when I fear not the axe itself?' he enquired. 'What dost thou fear?' The executioner was totally unnerved by the victim's calm demeanour and required two swings of the axe to sever the head from the body when urged by the prisoner, 'Strike, man, strike!'

Shunned at court, Stucley died a recluse on the remote isle of Lundy after finding there was no welcome for him in his native county. Calling on old Armada hero Lord Charles Howard of Effingham, he was turned away in no uncertain terms: 'How dare you come into my presence when you have gained the common scorn and contempt of all men. Were it not my own house, I would cudgel you with my staff for presuming to speak to me'. Stucley received no sympathy when he complained about Howard's manner to King James. 'What should I do with him? Hang him? On my soul, if I hung all that spoke ill of you, all the trees in the land would be too few.'

The Duke of Monmouth: The Pitchfork Rebellion

Monmouth's ambitions have now ended,
Since they seized his royal grace,
And his person they attended,
To a more secure place:
After that to London City,
Where on Tower Hill he died,
All his friends were moved with pity,
While his foes were satisfied.

Lines from contemporary ballad 'Monmouth Worsted in the West'.

In February 1685, a national crisis was created by the death of King Charles II as he left no legitimate heir. James Scott, the Duke of Monmouth, was the eldest of several children conceived by the king's numerous mistresses, but his claims to the throne were ignored as Charles' younger brother James II overcame Parliament's concerns about his conversion to the Roman Catholic faith and was granted the succession.

Urged on by his Protestant supporters, Monmouth mounted an ill-fated challenge to wrest the crown from his uncle. With money raised from pawning the jewellery of his mistress, Lady Wentworth, the Monmouth Rebellion began in June 1685 with less than 100 men. These ranks swelled within a week to an estimated 4,000 when supporters in the West Country answered the call to arms. Recruitment began when Monmouth sailed from Holland. He landed

The Duke of Monmouth.

at Lyme Regis before crossing the border from Dorset into East Devon, stopping at Axminster where he added to his force 'a great number of sober and pious men'.

The Devon Militia, mustered from Exeter to crush the rebellion, was led by Monmouth's old friend the Duke of Albermarle, who received a letter from his 'cousin' proclaiming himself to be 'head of and captain-general of the Protestant forces of this kingdom'. Sympathetic to the 'enemy', some militiamen deserted to join the cause, whilst the remainder did nothing to impede the progress of 'King Monmouth' and dropped back to shadow from a safe distance after almost crossing the path of the marching invasion force.

The Duke of Monmouth had been rapturously received during a tour of the South West five years earlier, visiting prominent towns and cities including Exeter – where reportedly about 1,000 'stout young men' greeted him. It was natural that he should return to the area for support in his foolhardy enterprise. Humble country folk happily supplied the charismatic Duke with information, fighting men and provisions. The 'pitchfork rising' of tradesmen and farmers were largely non-conformist Puritan 'dissenters' opposed to both the Anglican church and the papist monarch but ill-equipped for war. Crucially, they did not have the support of the local gentry, who were afraid to openly display what the Bishop of Exeter condemned as 'Hellish treason'. Consequently, when the rebels were intercepted in Somerset by the king's forces, the undisciplined ragbag army of yeomen were overrun at the Battle of Sedgemoor. Supplementing the royal army were regiments loaned by William of Orange, the king's son-in-law, who had his own designs on the Crown of England and would land at Brixham three years later to successfully depose King James II.

Rebel supporters of the vanquished Duke of Monmouth fled from the battlefield and sought sanctuary in the West Country. The government ordered them to be hunted down and brought before the notorious Judge George Jeffries. Trials held in courts on the Western Circuit at Dorchester, Exeter, Taunton and Wells became infamous as the 'Bloody Assizes'. At Exeter Assizes the judge immediately ordered the execution of three men who had the temerity to plead innocence. Sentence of death was deferred on the remainder who admitted their guilt having been promised leniency for co-operating. However, this proved a false hope as they were denied the 'king's mercy', and ten more were hanged, drawn and quartered, whilst the remainder were exiled to penal servitude in the West Indies, transported there on the optimistically named slave ship *Happy Return*.

Judge Jeffries.

With half of his force cut to pieces, the defeated Duke of Monmouth was pursued and caught hiding in a ditch, disguised as a peasant, in the New Forest. The 'Protestant Prince' tried to obtain belated favour from his uncle by offering to become a Catholic, but having had a price put on his head for declaring himself king, he was advised by the Earl of Dartmouth that a pardon was out of the question. Denied a trial, he was taken to Tower Hill where a shocked audience watched in horror as he was dispatched in grisly fashion by notorious executioner Jack Ketch. According to an eyewitness, the axe-man failed with five attempts to decapitate the prisoner and 'severed not his head from his body till he cut it off with his knife'.

The Western Rebellion had been savagely crushed, but the Duke quickly became a folk hero and within days of his unfortunate death, rumours began to circulate that he had avoided capture, and that the man who had been beheaded was one of five men chosen before Sedgemoor to impersonate Monmouth in order to confuse the enemy. Furthermore, having escaped from the battlefield it was only a matter of time before he would 'come again'. According to a contemporary account, it was popularly believed among common folk that 'the Duke of Monmouth is not really dead, but only withdrawn until the harvest is over, and then his friends shall see him again in a much better condition than ever they did yet'.

Chapter Four

Fraudsters

This image represents the confidence tricks of professional beggar Bampfylde Carew; corrupt politician Thomas Benson, bankrupt inventor Charles De Ville Wells and a woman who preyed on the families of dead war heroes, Maria Williams, are also in this chapter.

Bampfylde Moore Carew: King of the Beggars

King Carew's race at length is run,
His wanderings are all o'er;
No more his tricks, nor wit, nor fun,
Will make the table roar.
Bickleigh churchyard is now his home,
Peace rests upon him there;
And when the final day is come,
May he no danger fear!

From pamphlet *The Life and Adventures of Bamfylde Moore Carew.*

Of gentle birth, Bamfylde Moore Carew was named after his aristocratic godfathers, the Hon. Hugh Bampfylde and the Hon. Major Moore, and raised in Bickleigh (where his father, Theodore Carew, was rector for many years). In 1705, at the age of twelve, the boy was sent to complete his education at the famed Blundell's School in Tiverton, where fate intervened to lead him into a career far removed from the one he was being prepared for in his privileged upbringing at 'The Eton of the West'.

At the age of fifteen, Bampfylde and three of his schoolmates upset some local farmers by hunting on their land and damaging crops. Afraid to face the punishment that awaited them at the hands of their ferocious birch-wielding headmaster, the youths ran away and a chance encounter with a band of gypsies persuaded them to take up a nomadic life of freedom and idleness at the expense of others from whom they begged or stole. Gypsies were then regarded as worthless thieves and vagabonds and Carew soon displayed a natural flair for a life of crime. A master of disguise, Carew soon learned how to ensnare and deceive gullible victims for financial gain. In pursuit of these ends, the impostor regularly gained the public's sympathy (and relieved them of their money) by passing himself off in a variety of different personages including an elderly beggar woman, a young homeless mother with child, a shipwrecked mariner, an impoverished man whose possessions had been lost in a house fire, a farmer whose cattle had been drowned in a flood, a clergyman who had fallen on hard

Bampfylde Moore Carew.

Carew disguised as an old beggar woman.

times, and, often covering his modesty with no more than an old worn blanket, as the poor and demented 'Mad Tom'. Oddly, the only honest trade that the scoundrel ever learned was that of rat catcher, a service he enjoyed providing for his own community and the general public alike.

After eighteen months on the road, Carew was persuaded to return home by his heartbroken parents, but their comfortable lifestyle no longer suited their errant son and following a brief family reunion he slipped away at night without saying his farewells. Marriage was also attained using his skills of impersonation. Whilst visiting Newcastle, he fell in love with the daughter of an apothecary and surgeon and, with the captain's connivance, told her he was the mate of the vessel upon which they eloped to Dartmouth. Upon learning the truth about her suitor, the young lady happily entered into long and contented life of wedded bliss. Life seemed complete when Carew's reputation earned him the admiration of his fellow ne'er-do-wells, who bestowed upon him the coveted title 'King of the Gypsies'. However, trials and tribulations interrupted the rascal's career when he was convicted of vagrancy and transported into slavery on a plantation in Maryland. A bold bid for freedom involved having his shackles removed by Native Americans, swimming the Delaware River, then, in the guise of a Quaker, making his way via New York and Philadelphia to Boston where, having little money, he embarked for England and was paid for the trouble, having gained a berth as ship's mate. When he arrived home, his problems were far from over, for he was press-ganged to join the crew of a man-of-war, then immediately regained his liberty when he convinced his captors that he was suffering with deadly smallpox – an appearance brought about by pricking his hands and face with a pin, then rubbing salt and gunpowder into the bleeding wounds.

His American adventure over, Carew traced his wife and child and continued his life of deception for many years before winning a valuable prize in a lottery. This gave him the means to resettle in Bickleigh, where he died in contented idleness, at the age of sixty-six, in 1759. A legendary figure long before his death, further income had been obtained to provide comforts in retirement when the rogue's adventures were published in several editions chronicling exploits for which, unable to break the habits of a lifetime, he insincerely expressed remorse in *An Apology for the Life of Mr Bampfylde Moore Carew*.

One of the many editions of the beggar's adventures.

Thomas Benson: Crime Lord of Lundy

Thomas Benson won a contract,
To transport convicts overseas.
He landed them on Lundy,
Sailing only two or three leagues.
Living on the island,
The men were treated like slaves.
Concealing contraband,
Deep inside the smuggler's caves.

Verse by Mike Holgate.

Lying in the Bristol Channel, twelve miles off the coast of Devon, the 'tempestuous isle' of Lundy was for centuries the perfect lair of pirates including Norman knight Sir William De Marisco, corsairs from the Barbary Coast and the notorious buccaneer Captain Kidd (who was reputed to have hidden buried treasure on what was commonly known as 'Pirate Island').

Finally freed of life under the black flag, the uninhabited Lundy was acquired by an outwardly respectable Bideford merchant and former High Sheriff of Devon, Thomas Benson. In 1748, the forty-year-old recently elected Member of Parliament for Barnstaple took up residence in the island castle – which he then used as a power base for various devious criminal activities involving breach of contract, smuggling, tax evasion and insurance fraud. Pulling parliamentary strings, the shipowner was awarded a government contract to transport convicts to the American penal colonies of Maryland and Virginia. However, a significant number of the fittest and most skilled members of the human cargo were landed on Lundy and never saw the New World. The island castle served as a prison for the convicts, who were well fed with readily available deer, goats, wildfowl and rabbits hunted on land, and plentiful crab, lobster and fish caught from the sea. In return for their accommodation, the men provided a captive labour force, cultivating and improving the island by working on the land and in the quarries. When Benson's vessels returned to North Devon from America they imported tobacco which was

A map of Lundy.

unloaded on the island to avoid customs duty. The contraband was stored in 'Benson's Cave' situated beneath the castle. It was excavated with convict labour, enlarging an existing grotto. Cut deep into the rock, measuring 72ft long, 10ft wide with a height of 7ft and an entrance formed by a massive slab of rock resting on two uprights, it provided the perfect hiding place for concealing the crime lord's ill-gotten goods.

Benson's duplicity was uncovered when eight prisoners escaped in a longboat to Hartland, and the officers of the Collector

Lundy Castle.

of Customs for Barnstaple raided the island and seized a large quantity of illegally imported tobacco. Benson was heavily fined for defrauding the government of customs dues, but refused to pay: a warrant was issued for the appropriation of his North Devon estate to cover the cost of the penalties imposed. With regard to the convicts, the culprit avoided prosecution by arguing, improbably, that he had abided with his contract to the letter of the law, claiming that travelling to Lundy was 'overseas' as it was 'out of the kingdom'. In fact, Benson had made no secret of the prisoner's destination when he brazenly invited a group of guests, including Sir Thomas Gunson, the Sheriff of Somerset, to inspect his stronghold. However, having now lost his lands and lucrative means of income, Benson tried to recoup his losses by planning an insurance fraud that resulted in tragedy. He arranged for a valuable cargo to be unloaded on Lundy, and then ordered his brigantine *Nightingale* to be sailed over the horizon and scuttled. The captain and crew took to the boats and were picked up by a homeward-bound ship. An inflated insurance claim for the sunken vessel and its 'lost' cargo was then submitted, but with so many people involved in the scam, it wasn't long before the truth leaked out and the law was set in motion.

The ship's master, Captain John Lancey of Bideford, was arrested, summarily tried by the Admiralty Court in London and hanged at Execution Dock in June 1754. Leaving the luckless Lancey to his fate, Benson had avoided capture by galloping on horseback from Bideford to Plymouth. Fleeing from justice, with funds raised from selling the illicit cargo deposited on Lundy, he secured a passage to Portugal. Feeling homesick, he bided his time until the scandal died down, then returned in disguise to his hometown, where he was soon recognised visiting his old haunts. Rather than risk arrest and the certainty of the death penalty, Thomas Benson was forced back into exile and the felon ended his days in Portugal in 1771. Thenceforth, the isle of Lundy lived down its dark past and enjoyed a more peaceful existence, thanks mainly to the efforts of William Hudson Heaven and his son, the aptly named Reverend Hudson Grosett Heaven. The former purchased the island in 1834 and it passed to the priest in 1883, who oversaw the building of a church, completed in 1896. This prompted a visit from the Bishop of Exeter, who wryly observed, after a rough sea crossing, that he had passed through Purgatory to arrive at the 'Kingdom of Heaven'.

Captain Lancey and his crew leave the scuttled *Nightingale*.

Charles De Ville Wells: The Man Who Broke the Bank at Monte Carlo

As I walk along the Bois Boolong with an independent air,
I can hear the girls declare 'he must be a millionaire'.
You can hear them sigh and wish to die,
You can see them wink the other eye,
At the man who broke the bank at Monte Carlo.

Chorus of music-hall song 'The Man Who Broke the Bank at Monte Carlo' by Fred Gilbert.

Fraudster and gambler Charles De Ville Wells, immortalised in the popular music-hall song as 'the man who broke the bank at Monte Carlo', was born at Broxbourne, Hertfordshire in 1841, the son of lawyer and poet Charles Jeremiah Wells. The family relocated to France, where Charles junior finalised his education in Marseilles before pursuing various business interests across Europe. Having disposed of a successful company in Paris, he returned to England in 1885 with a capital of £8,000, a cash sum which was soon exhausted. While residing in Plymouth, he determined to become a successful inventor and provisionally applied for almost 200 patents. These included an idea to radically improve the efficiency of steam engines that was to bring about his downfall.

Taking out advertisements in the press to attract investors to back his invention in return for a share of fabulous profits, Wells acquired the necessary capital to fit out six vessels at Plymouth. The pride of the fleet was the luxury yacht *Palais Royal*, which boasted a ballroom, music room and sumptuous accommodation for sixty guests, necessary, the investors were assured, as a showpiece to promote the new and improved engine. In July 1891, the inventor 'tested' the vessel while sailing in the Mediterranean. Accompanied by a mistress thirty years his junior, the beautiful artist's model Jeanette Paris, the yacht called at Monte Carlo. From this moment on, business was to become secondary to gambling, for Wells enjoyed extraordinary luck at the roulette wheel. Boldly placing even money bets on red and black, he won

Monte Carlo, 1891.

on virtually every spin of the wheel until he finally exceeded the 100,000 francs 'bank' allocated to each table. On these extremely rare occasions, attendants ceremoniously covered the table with a black 'mourning' cloth and closed it for business for the rest of the day, signifying that the 'bank' was temporarily 'broken'. However, this was to be no fluke by Wells, who during a five-day spree broke the bank a total of twelve times. At one stage he won twenty-three times out of thirty spins of the wheel and sailed away with £40,000. These extraordinary feats of good fortune at the roulette wheel gained the winner celebrity status in the press, and before long, music-hall star Charles Coburn was featuring a song written by Fred Gilbert inspired by the gambler's success. Whenever Wells entered a nightclub or restaurant, the orchestra would strike up his signature tune, 'The Man Who Broke the Bank at Monte Carlo'.

Wells triumphed at the tables again in November 1891, raising another fortune of £20,000. However, his gambler's 'courage' was tested to the limit when he returned to Monte Carlo for a third time in October 1892. The winning 'system' – whose principle he claimed to have discovered while developing his wondrous fuel-saving engine – finally failed him. His amazing run of luck came to a ruinous end as he began to lose, lose, lose. He gambled every penny he had – what remained of his previous winnings and the money invested in his company – before trying to win it back with further cash he persuaded his investors to part with, on the pretext that his yacht had caught fire and expensive 'repairs' had to be made to his fuel-saving engine. Doubling his stake to recoup his losses had disastrous results, compounding his reversal of fortune.

By the time the *Palais Royal* sailed home and anchored in Plymouth Sound, proceedings to sue the yacht's owner had been instigated to recover monies owed to bilked investors. 'Monte Carlo' Wells fled to France, but was extradited to 'face the music' in London at the Old Bailey and was jailed for eight years on charges of fraud in March 1893. When the bankrupt swindler was granted remission and released in March 1899, he changed his name to Charles Davenport and, with Jeanette Paris (posing as 'Mrs Davenport'), settled in Cork – where he subsequently hatched another scheme which landed him back in court in November 1905. He was charged with obtaining £6,000 from investors in a bogus company – the South & South-West Coasts Steam Trawling Fishing Syndicate – which, in actuality, owned two steam launches and only one trawler which was not even seaworthy. Committed for trial on charges of 'conspiracy to defraud and obtaining money by false pretences and obtaining credit while an undischarged bankrupt', Wells received three further years of imprisonment. Paroled after serving only half of his

Plymouth Sound.

sentence, Wells entered into matrimony with his long-time lover Jeanette, and the pair formed a criminal partnership, culminating in the robbery of their own bank!

In July 1910, Wells adopted the name Lucien Rivier and opened a bogus bank in Paris offering to pay 1% a day interest to investors – equivalent to a too-good-to-be-true annual return of 365%. Over a period of eight months, 60,000 people were taken in by the scam, investing a total of £120,000 and attracted by a circular which boasted, 'There may exist firms which guarantee no loss in Stock Exchange transactions; ours is the only one which assures a constant daily profit'. Predictably, the shady bank suddenly closed for business and the couple took off with their ill-gotten gains in a newly acquired luxury yacht named *Harbinger* and anchored off the coast of Falmouth. The money swindled from investors was placed in bank accounts opened in the names of Charles and Janet De Ville, but the long arm of international law eventually caught up with the fugitives, who were detained by a police officer from Scotland Yard in January 1912. Following a protracted and unsuccessful appeal against extradition proceedings, seventy-year-old Wells was forced to return to France and face justice for his latest crime spree. The trial resulted in a further period of imprisonment for five years on charges of fraudulent bankruptcy and obtaining money by false pretences. Charles De Ville Wells was buried in a pauper's grave when he passed away in 1926. Celebrated in life as the man who broke the bank, the incorrigible fraudster met his maker broke and utterly bankrupt in Paris.

Maria Williams: Swindling the Mother of Rex Warneford, VC

The mother of a war hero,
A highly decorated airman,
Was the victim of a confidence trick
Played by a heartless woman.

Verse by Mike Holgate.

Reginald 'Rex' Warneford began a career in the merchant navy at the age of thirteen, but at the outbreak of the First World War was rejected for the submarine service at Britannia Royal Naval College, Dartmouth. After a brief spell in the Sportsman's Battalion, he transferred to the Royal Naval Air Service and in June 1915, only four months after completing his training, the twenty-three-year-old Flight Sub-Lieutenant became the first airman in history to destroy a Zeppelin in flight.

Whilst flying on patrol he located an enemy airship and shadowed it from Flanders to its base near Ghent. As the heavily armed quarry glided into land, Warneford swooped in for the attack and, hovering less than 200ft above the target, dropped a full load of six bombs. The first five penetrated the Zeppelin and exploded harmlessly before the final one had the desired effect, igniting inside the 600ft-long craft and killing all twenty-eight members of the crew, who either fell to their deaths or were burned alive in a ball of fire. Sadly, the flaming wreckage also showered down on a convent, resulting in the loss of innocent lives. The victorious pilot felt shockwaves from the blast which blew his aeroplane into a spin; his engine stopped, forcing him to make an emergency landing in hostile territory. Quickly repairing a fractured fuel line, he successfully restarted his engine and flew

Rex Warneford, VC.

to safety just as a group of German soldiers closed in and opened fire with rifles and machine guns.

Within thirty-six hours of this thrilling deed, Warneford received a telegram from King George V: 'I most heartily congratulate you upon your splendid achievement of yesterday, in which you single-handedly destroyed an enemy Zeppelin. I have much pleasure in conferring upon you the Victoria Cross for this gallant act'. Warneford was the first officer of the Royal Naval Air

Service to be so honoured, but instead of returning to England he travelled to Paris to receive another decoration, the Cross of the Legion of Honour. Fêted in the French capital, he agreed to take an American journalist for a test flight in a brand-new aeroplane. Soon after taking off, the aircraft suddenly spiralled out of control and broke up in the air. Not wearing their safety straps, the two occupants were flung out of the cockpit. The passenger died instantly, whilst the pilot suffered grievous injuries. Rex Warneford passed away in a military hospital having enjoyed just ten days of fame. At his funeral at Brompton Cemetery in London, 50,000 people turned out to pay homage to the fallen hero. On his coffin was a wreath in the form of an aeroplane with the Victoria Cross and the Cross of the Legion of Honour on each wing. Attached to the wreath was a ribbon bearing the inscription, 'Honoured by the King, admired by the Empire, but mourned by all'.

It was reported that, on the day before his death, Warneford had been presented with a bunch of roses in a restaurant and someone commented, 'What rejoicings there will be when you return to England to see your mother again'. To this the young officer chillingly prophesied, 'I feel that I shall die before I return home'.

Born in India, where his father worked as a civil engineer, Rex Warneford's parents had parted when he was a youngster. Subsequently his father died, and his mother remarried. She became Mrs Alexandra Corkery, living at Exmouth in Devon. A few months after her son's death she became the victim of a cruel confidence trick perpetrated by Maria Fenton Williams: the fraudster called at her house falsely claiming that she was an artist whose own son had been killed at the front. The heartless woman obtained money from Mrs Corkery after offering to paint three oil paintings of her heroic son. She was arrested after supplying tinted colour copies of the photographs loaned to her by her trusting client. Williams pleaded 'not guilty' but was fined £2 for obtaining money under false pretences and, as she left the court, was immediately rearrested for committing a similar offence in Torquay.

Housekeeper Elizabeth Squires had been visited at her place of employment by the accused and parted with a cash deposit in exchange for oil paintings of the son she had recently lost. The order was placed but she never received the pictures, nor the return of her money and the three photographs she had provided for the 'artist' to draw a likeness of the deceased soldier. In evidence given at Torquay Magistrates Court, it emerged that bereaved parents in Ideford, Newton Abbot and Kingsteignton had also fallen for the scam. Williams won their sympathy with imaginary sob stories, pretending that her son had died fighting for the Devon Regiment and that she was a poor widow left with an invalid daughter to care for. Despite the defendant's solicitor claiming that his client had simply been unable to deliver the oil paintings on time due to the large amount of orders she had received, Williams was jailed for six weeks and the chairman of the bench remarked that the charge of false pretences had been justly proven and the crime was 'a cold-blooded and callous attempt to take advantage of other people'.

Meanwhile, Alexandra Corkery had some consolation when she received the prized decoration awarded to her son from the Admiralty and on 5 October, the day after her upsetting court appearance in Exmouth, the king wrote her a letter saying that it was a matter of sincere regret that the death of the officer had 'deprived him of the pride of personally conferring upon him the Victoria Cross, the greatest of all naval distinctions'.

Chapter Five

Dartmoor Escapes

Daring plans to escape from prison ended in recapture for John Gasken and
George Whitehead, and the tragic deaths of William Carter and Frank Mitchell.

William Carter: Death on the Moor

Sometimes when things are very dull, a convict makes a dash,
To gain his freedom, but the guards of him soon make a hash.
Lag-shooting is such a good old sport it's never out of season,
But to shoot a pheasant in July is almost worse than treason.

From Dartmoor Prison poem, *Lay of the Lagged Minstrel by An Old Lag.*

During the Victorian era, Dartmoor Prison at Princetown had a reputation among hardened criminals as being the most inhospitable place in which to serve 'time'. Many desperate convicts found ways to escape from the confines of the prison, but few made it to freedom beyond the bleak moorland. Prisoners on the run had many obstacles to overcome: the grim weather; swirling mists that could envelope the landscape and reduce visibility to zero in seconds; treacherous bogs where many 'successful' escapees may have been sucked to their deaths; sharp-eyed local people known as 'five-pounders' eager to claim a £5 reward for apprehending a fleeing villain. Fugitives also risked death at the hands of their armed pursuers, who would shoot to kill.

One such tragedy occurred just before noon on Christmas Eve 1896, when three men made a run from a work party reclaiming

A work party passing through the prison gate.

William Carter was shot as he leapt over a low wall.

bogland near the Blackabrook River. The chief instigator of the escape plan was twenty-two year old William Carter, who had been recently parted from his new bride to serve a twelve-year sentence for robbery with violence. His co-conspirators were Ralph Goodwin and John Martin, both serving long sentences for burglary. During the onset of a heavy rainfall, a dense mist descended and visibility deteriorated rapidly; work was abandoned, and the armed escort ordered the party to march back to the prison. On a signal from Carter, earth was thrown into the faces of the guards and the trio dashed for the cover of some woodland. As he leapt over a low wall, the unfortunate Carter was cut down by a hail of bullets and died instantly, while Martin was quickly overpowered and knocked cold with a truncheon.

Meanwhile, Goodwin vanished into the mist and spent the rest of the day trying to put as much distance as possible between himself and Princetown. Suffering from exposure as the wind and torrential rain swept across the moor, the worst weather experienced in the locality for years, the fleeing convict fell into the water three times as he stumbled along the bank of a swollen river. As dawn broke, the tired and hungry convict was dismayed to discover that he had travelled in a complete circle and arrived back within sight of the prison. Tempted to give himself up, but worried he might suffer the same fate as Carter, he set out again and made good progress on Christmas Day. At one point he was spotted by a distant search party and gave them a cheeky wave of his hat before disappearing from view. That night he broke into two houses at Postbridge and obtained a change of clothes. On Boxing Day he reached Tavistock and raided another house, hungrily helping himself to half a cooked turkey, two plum puddings, several eggs and a loaf of bread before spending the night trudging along the railway track towards Plymouth. When challenged by a team of gangers carrying out maintenance work on the track, he told them he stood to win a bet of £5 by walking from Tiverton to Plymouth.

Reaching Devonport and wandering near the Royal Naval Dockyards, a successful getaway was within Goodwin's grasp when his life-on-the-run came to an end. At 6 a.m., he met dog handler PC Prestwood and wished him 'Good morning' without arousing suspicion, then, when the policeman's fox terrier ran playfully after him across the road, he believed he had been rumbled, lost his nerve and ran. The exhausted fugitive was chased by the constable and quickly cornered. Standing against a wall he flashed a stolen cheese knife at his pursuer and shouted, 'Stand back or I'll stab you'. The police officer calmly out-bluffed his assailant by pretending to reach for a revolver in his pocket, which, he threatened, he would have no hesitation in using unless the desperate criminal gave himself up. Goodwin dropped the weapon and surrendered. Escorted by six armed guards, he returned

William Carter at the time of his arrest.

to Dartmoor, where any vestige of festive spirit among the inmates had been quashed by the death of William Carter. At the subsequent inquest, held at Princetown, Ralph Goodwin and John Martin were both of the opinion that the deceased could have been apprehended without resorting to the use of firearms, whereas the prison officials considered that under the circumstances, it was their duty to shoot him down. Principal Warder Rowe, who, on the fateful day, had been in charge of the work party of fifty-eight convicts, testified that he shouted three warnings to the escapees. When they refused to halt, he gave the other guards an order to open fire. As a result, William Carter's untimely death was caused by thirteen bullet wounds in the back. There was applause from the public gallery when the jury returned a unanimous verdict of 'justifiable homicide'.

George Whitehead: Joyride to Freedom

Sunday morning when we've breakfasted, we march away to chapel,
The chaplain says we are all lagged because Eve stole an apple.
We sing and pray all out of tune and then we kneel and pray,
And hear a cheer to signal that some lag's got away.

From Dartmoor Prison poem, *Lay of the Lagged Minstrel by An Old Lag*.

In April 1928, a correspondent of the Torquay newspaper *Herald & Express* reported:

The daring escape from Princetown Prison, Dartmoor, described only a short time ago by the Home Secretary, Sir Joynsen Hicks, as 'the cesspool of humanity', by George Whitehead, who was undergoing a sentence of seven years' penal servitude, has many of the features of Mr John Galsworthy's remarkable play, *Escape*... For rapidity of action, and cool calculation, the escape is unequalled in the history of Princetown.

A former Torquay garage owner, George Whitehead, one of the many aliases of car thief Robert Smith, used a combination of his professional and criminal skills to become the first convict to escape from Dartmoor Prison in a motor vehicle. On Sunday mornings, Whitehead was exempted from attending chapel service because he had a job as bathhouse attendant, cleaning the communal washrooms of the penal institution. From 10.30–11.30 a.m., the prisoner was locked in the room to carry out his duties – but on this occasion, when the warders returned, they found the place mysteriously deserted.

Whitehead had cunningly gained his liberty by removing slates from the roof of the bathhouse, scaling the high prison wall by means of a ladder, cutting the telephone wires connecting the prison with the telephone exchange, dodging under cover of a dense mist through a field across the main road, then raiding a garage almost within a stone's throw of the main entrance of the prison to steal an open-top Clyno two-seater car belonging to Roman Catholic priest Father Flanagan. Cheekily, instead of making off across the moor, the fleeing prisoner drove down the main street of Princetown, where the village constable, assuming

A car similar to the one stolen is stopped at a police roadblock on Dartmoor.

the vehicle was occupied by its rightful owner, gave the driver a polite salute!

When the alarm was sounded, the police were summoned and immediately realised that the fugitive would be heading towards his home in Torquay, where his wife had given birth to their first child, whom the father had never seen. Quickly on the trail, police officers found the stolen car stuck in the mud and abandoned eighteen miles away at Dartington. In torrential rain, Whitehead then evidently tramped more than ten miles to Paignton and, late at night, broke into the garage of a local dentist and stole the gentleman's brand-new brown Morris Oxford saloon. Driving along the seafront, he reached his destination of Torquay. Stopping off to steal cigarettes, chocolates, milk and clothes from a café on Meadfoot Beach leased by local celebrity and former Olympic diver 'Tack' Collings, he parked for the night in the wealthy residential area known as 'Millionaire's Row' on Marine Drive. At 6 a.m. the next morning, the owner of one of the villas noticed that the driver was asleep on the back seat of the car and went out to investigate. The startled fugitive awoke and threw off a blanket, revealing a glimpse of his prison uniform under a stolen raincoat. Pretending not to notice, the gentleman hurried off to telephone the police as the wary convict drove away.

Detective Sergeant Gill and Detective Drew, who had been up all night searching for the fugitive, responded to the call and drove to the spot where their quarry had spent the night. Examining the scene, they noticed a perfect impression of the saloon's new tyres and certain distinctive features about it. Carefully following the tracks, they saw that the car was heading in the direction of Newton Abbot before losing the trail. After considering the situation, the detectives deduced that Whitehead was probably travelling on a back road where he might hide out until nightfall. Their hunch proved correct, for soon they came across the distinctive tyre marks they had been following and were on the 'scent' again. The trail led along an extremely muddy, rain sodden lane that led to the secluded village of Coffinswell. Before long they became bogged down in the mud and could travel no further, but after alighting from the vehicle, they walked around the next bend and came across their man attempting to

'Tack' Collings giving a diving display at Torquay.

jack up his stolen vehicle, which had sunk in the mud right up to the axles. The convict immediately ran off, jumped over a gate and began sprinting across a field. Although Whitehead was a violent criminal who had served just over two years of a seven-year sentence for shooting at a policeman in Blackpool, where he had driven in a car stolen from Torquay, Gill and Drew did not hesitate in giving chase and within seconds had cornered the runaway who, following a brief struggle, was overpowered and handcuffed. Taken to Torquay police station, Whitehead was allowed to see his wife, who had been too ill to visit him following the birth of their child. She told the press, 'He said he could not resist coming to see us when the car was left unattended. Although I was angry with him I was pleased to see him even under such circumstances'. However, the proud father did not seem so pleased when a local reporter suggested to the exhausted, wet, bedraggled prisoner, 'I should think you are glad to be captured', to which Whitehead angrily replied, 'Glad! I am anything but glad. I wish somebody had shot me instead of capturing me!'

John Gasken: The Double Escapee

I'm doing five long weary years at Dartmoor wild and bleak,
Of what I've suffered, seen and heard, I really cannot speak,
So when the opportunity comes I'm going to take my chance
To run away and lead the screws on a merry dance.

Adapted from Dartmoor Prison poem, *Lay of the Lagged Minstrel* by *An Old Lag*.

Despite Dartmoor being the setting for Arthur Conan Doyle's fictional *The Hound of the Baskervilles*, the titular hound that attacked and killed an escaped convict, dogs were not used to track down fugitives until 1931. On Friday 6 February of that year, two men working in the stone sheds scaled a 32ft wall with the aid of a rope to which was attached a grappling hook. The fugitives were John Mullins, aged twenty-eight, a native of York serving a sentence of three years for a housebreaking offence committed in 1929. During the First World War he had served in France with his fellow escapee, John Gasken, aged thirty-one, also of York, who had completed only six months of a five-year sentence for housebreaking, forgery and false pretences. While serving a previous period of incarceration in November 1921, Gasken had boldly walked out of Birmingham Prison wearing a warder's uniform.

Instead of blindly heading out across the moor in the thick fog, the duo cleverly followed a leat leading to Burrator Reservoir. The next day they stole food and a change of clothing from two unoccupied houses near the railway station at Yelverton. By now, three bloodhounds loaned from kennels at Liskeard had picked up the scent and were hot on the trail, but the hunt was called off after the eldest dog collapsed, exhausted, after five hours on the run.

Bloodhounds on the scent of John Gasken.

On Sunday morning, Mullins was recaptured on the outskirts of Plymouth after the fugitives had become separated. Gasken remained at liberty for a further two days. During Monday, he sold a stolen jumper at a second-hand shop and bought himself a cup of tea and two pasties before spending the day at a branch library, where he read about the hue and cry for his capture. He was finally apprehended near the locomotive depot at Laira on the outskirts of Plymouth. Hoping to board a goods train to Bristol, he walked along the track using a stolen torch. Along the way he had spoken to some railway workers who mistakenly presumed he was a railway detective searching for the escaped convict. With the bloodhounds closing in and baying loudly in the distance, a policeman saw Gasken entering an office in the railway siding. When challenged, Gasken claimed his name was Brooks and that he had just arrived from Southampton and was waiting to board a boat at Plymouth. His story was not believed, and he was detained and questioned by a suspicious Detective-Inspector Lucas: 'I believe your name is Gasken and that you are missing from your home on Dartmoor'. Still refusing to accept that the game was up, Gasken replied innocently, 'Where is Dartmoor?' 'You will know soon enough,' was the confident reply, and after vainly protesting, 'You are making the worst mistake you ever made in your life', Gasken finally dropped the pretence and admitted he was the missing convict adding, 'I am hungry and fed up'.

John Gasken's five days at liberty had taken its toll on his health and he was confined in the prison hospital having developed pneumonia. After his capture, he told police, 'I didn't know what Dartmoor was like – I'll never try it again' – yet within two years he was on the run again. This attempt was made in November 1932 while Gasken, accompanied by London burglar Frederick Amy, was carrying out repairs to the roof of some cells. The men utilised a ladder, thoughtlessly left unsupervised for their building work, to scale a 15ft wall to the outside. Although never venturing more than thirty miles from the prison, Gasken and Amy established a record for escaped Dartmoor convicts and were at liberty for six days before their recapture. Neither man had been involved in the infamous Dartmoor Mutiny in January of that year, when prisoners planned a mass breakout. The attempt was made and thwarted as 350 men were being escorted to a Sunday chapel service. The prisoners then went on the rampage for an hour, vandalising and burning prison buildings. Many surrendered and quietly returned to their cells before the hardcore rebels were finally brought under control when forty policemen, drafted in from Plymouth, charged with drawn batons. Security had supposedly been stepped up following this incident, which attracted national headlines, so the escape of Amy and Gasken was an added embarrassment for the prison authorities.

Bloodhounds were brought from Shaugh Prior, but the hunt was temporarily called off at nightfall. Meanwhile, the fugitives made their way towards the railway at Horrabridge Station and on Thursday night broke into the booking office and took oilskin coats. The robbery was discovered at 6 a.m., and the bloodhounds soon picked up the trail. They followed it along the railway line in the direction of Tavistock until the scent deviated to the moor, where it was lost amongst a flock of sheep. Gasken and Amy laid low during the day and then completed their chosen route along the railway track to Tavistock, where they joined the line at Lydford. Gasken, who realised that he would be expected to retrace his earlier escape to Plymouth, had decided to try his

Gasken, the only inmate to escape twice from Dartmoor.

luck in the opposite direction, walking from Lydford to Exeter. Throughout the weekend the police searched in vain for the two men. According to the convicts, at one point the bloodhounds came within a few yards of their hiding place and the fugitives stroked a small terrier accompanying the search party until it ran off, disinterested. Continuing their journey along the railway, they met a signalman and satisfied his curiosity by convincing him that they were seeking work. The net closed in when they broke into a house at Crediton and stole food, money and a change of clothes, leaving behind the oilskins. Late that night their record-breaking escape came to an end only twelve hours short of a full seven days at liberty. Spotted on the railway track on the outskirts of Exeter, they went quietly when approached by two policemen. The only inmate to escape twice from Dartmoor, John Gasken was normally one of the best-behaved men in the prison but could not resist the opportunity to outwit his captors when the chance presented itself to go on the run. When asked by a policeman if he was glad his latest escapade was over he replied ominously, 'Yes, but I didn't want it to end this way.'

Frank Mitchell: The Mad Axeman

We join our parties on parade each day when we've churched,
And lest a lag should conceal a chiv we're diligently searched.

When all's correct we march away in hail, rain, snow, or fog,
To practice agricultural work in trenching on the bog.

Adapted from Dartmoor Prison poem, *Lay of the Lagged Minstrel
by An Old Lag*.

Dartmoor Prison attracted lurid headlines when Frank 'Mad Axeman' Mitchell escaped from a working party at Peter Tavy, five miles from Tavistock. The violent former Rampton and Broadmoor mental patient had previously escaped from both institutions and once, whilst on the run, had robbed an elderly couple in their home after threatening them with an axe taken from their garden shed. The terrified victims were forced to watch television whilst their captor calmly drank a cup of tea with the axe resting on his knees – an episode that earned him the sobriquet 'The Mad Axeman'. For this crime he was sentenced to life imprisonment, charged with robbery with violence and with no fixed date for his release. Having served nine years, the thirty-seven-year-old with the mind of a child felt there was no hope of the Home Secretary considering his case; therefore, he took the opportunity offered by his gangland associates to secure his own freedom.

There was a national outcry when it was learned that such a dangerous career criminal was not incarcerated in a high-security prison. On two previous occasions he had been flogged for assaulting prison warders; therefore, questions were raised about his participation in 'honour parties' normally made up of non-violent prisoners coming to the end of their sentences. Furthermore, it transpired that despite the prisoner's nickname, the implement he was regularly provided with was an axe! However, Mitchell never did any work and had been allowed to wander away, unchallenged, from work parties and to roam the moor, where he had been known to regularly enjoy the hospitality of village pubs. Unbelievably, on one occasion he ordered a taxi, journeyed to Tavistock and purchased a budgerigar!

Following Mitchell's escape on 12 December 1966, one of the greatest manhunts in Dartmoor Prison's history was mounted. Moorland farmers were warned to lock their properties securely

Dartmoor Prison.

and the public instructed not to approach the fugitive. A senior police officer said: 'He is a dangerous man who will stop at nothing. He is not to be trifled with'. However, a local farmer revealed that he had met Mitchell many times and was far from afraid of him. The convict had often visited him to ride one of his moorland ponies, 'He was a jolly chap, very mild and pleasant. I knew all about him and that he was a prisoner'.

Police officers, prison warders and soldiers combed the area for 'the most dangerous criminal in England', a search that lasted for two days before the hunt was switched away from the moor. It was later learned that Mitchell had been immediately whisked away in a waiting car by members of the infamous Kray gang who controlled London's underworld in the 1960s. Plans had been laid by notorious twins Ronnie and Reggie, who corresponded with Mitchell. The latter also wore a disguise when making a prison visit to arrange a rendezvous on the moor. A few days after the escape, national newspapers received handwritten letters from the fugitive offering to give himself up if he was given hope of freedom:

> Sir, the reason for my absence from Dartmoor was to bring to the notice of my unhappy plight, to be truthful I am asking for a possible date of release. From the age of nine I have not been completely free, always [held] under some act or other.
>
> Sir, I ask you, where is the fairness of this? I am not a murderer or sex maniac nor do I think I am a danger to the

public. I think I have been more than punished for the wrongs I have done.

I am ready to give myself up if I can have something to look forward to. I do not intend to use any violence at any time should I be found, that is why I left a knife behind with my prison things.

The Home Secretary, reeling under a barrage of press criticism, refused to bow to such demands, which he felt were tantamount to blackmail; therefore, 'Big Frank' grew increasingly frustrated. He had been provided with female company in the shape of a nightclub hostess, but his liberators had now taken on the role of gaolers, keeping him cooped up inside a small flat. He became restless and annoyed that Ronnie and Reggie Kray weren't doing more to help him. Violent mood swings ensued as he alternated between hyperactive behaviour and bouts of depression. 'The Firm' suddenly felt threatened by his presence and decided to deal with their problem 'guest'. 'Mad Frank' was never recaptured, and what became of him was shrouded in mystery until the Kray brothers received sentences of life imprisonment for their criminal activities in 1969. At the trail, it was alleged that Mitchell had become troublesome to the gang and been killed on 23 December, less than two weeks after going on the run. The gangland brothers were cleared of this particular charge, but Reggie Kray later claimed in his autobiography that four men were paid to take Mitchell out of the country but, when he became difficult, they murdered him instead, shooting him three times. Contradicting this version of events, other criminal sources have claimed that orders from the 'terrible twins' brought about Mitchell's death. Three henchmen escorted 'Big Frank' to a van on the pretext that he was to be taken to spend Christmas with Ronnie Kray. Following a violent struggle, he was shot dead, although it took twelve bullets to finish him off. An unsubstantiated rumour persists that his corpse was then disposed of in a concrete mixer and poured into a pillar supporting a motorway bridge.

Chapter Six

Robbers

Legendary highwayman Tom Faggus, jewel thief Ethel Elliott and daring train
robbers Henry Poole and Bruce Reynolds all won public admiration and
sympathy for their criminal acts.

Tom Faggus: The Robin Hood of Exmoor

Tom Faggus was a bold highwayman,
The scourge of travellers in North Devon.
His life was shrouded in mystery,
Some say he died on the gallows tree.

From folk song *Tom Faggus* by Mike Holgate.

The adventures of Devon's most renowned highwayman Tom Faggus reached a wider audience when he featured as a central character in R.D. Blackmore's classic novel, *Lorna Doone*. In the story, Tom Faggus's daring feats on Exmoor astride his strawberry roan 'Winnie' are accurately described thus: 'A bold highwayman… who scoured these wastes on a steed as famous for his fleetness and sagacity, as his master was for a remarkable combination of audacity and benevolence. He did the knave good service in many a hard pinch, and carried him safely through such dangers imminent, that he was called "The Enchanted Strawberry Horse".'

TOM FAGGUS TOOK IT EAGERLY, AND BORE IT TO THE WINDOW.

Tom Faggus as portrayed in *Lorna Doone*.

Long Bridge, Barnstaple.

In the middle of the seventeenth century, Tom Faggus contentedly practiced his trade as a blacksmith at North Molton until he became embroiled in a lawsuit brought by the powerful and influential Bamfylde family of Court Hall. As a result of these rigged legal proceedings, the young blacksmith lost his lands and his business. His life took another turn for the worse when the father of his fiancée, Betsy Paramore of South Molton, refused to allow his daughter to marry such a poverty-stricken suitor. From this moment on, a resentful Tom Faggus vowed to gain recompense for perceived wrongs, turned to a life of crime and, in the tradition of an earlier legendary outlaw, Robin Hood, robbed only the rich and helped the poor.

Many are the tales of Tom Faggus's thrilling contests with the law. On one occasion, Faggus had taken refuge in a house in Porlock where he was surrounded by armed men. The posse were thwarted when their quarry thrust his hat on a stick through the chimney, drawing a volley of fire. Before the weapons could be reloaded, the front door flew open and Faggus was swiftly carried out of harm's way by his fleet-footed horse. The tightest spot that horse and rider found themselves in occurred on Long Bridge at Barnstaple: word had spread that the wanted man was approaching and every available constable was assembled to spring an ambush. As Winnie cantered unwittingly into the trap, both ends of the bridge were sealed off with a cordon of officers.

It seemed that every avenue of escape had been closed, but the quick-thinking highwayman urged his brave steed up onto the parapet of the bridge and the pair plunged down into the waters of the River Taw some 40ft below. To the dismay of the lawmen, Winnie then swam ashore, where Faggus cheerily doffed his sodden hat to the dumbfounded audience.

The intelligent mare once rescued her master by rearing to knock a cocked weapon from a would-be assailant's hand, but even her seemingly magical powers eventually failed. In Blackmore's fictional account, Tom Faggus receives a royal pardon, but it is commonly believed, although no proof has been found, that in real life, the law finally caught up with the highwayman in a tavern where he was overpowered by the constabulary, bound and strung upside down from the rafters. When the robber whistled to summon aid from his faithful steed, Winnie was shot dead by her master's captors. The heavily guarded Faggus was then escorted to Taunton, tried and hanged in 1671.

There is no doubt that the most satisfying moment of the highwayman's eventful career occurred when he encountered his arch-enemy, Bamfylde, the very man whose shenanigans in the law courts had reduced the young blacksmith to poverty. Facing a brace of pistols, the terrified Bamfylde promptly emptied his pockets and offered his money and valuables, then was surprised to be handed them back and told by the bandit, 'Permit me the pleasure, sir, of honouring the custom that a robber never robs a robber'.

Henry Poole: The Great Western Train Robbery

Late in the evening on New Year's Day,
A fortune in valuables went astray.
Poole and Nightingale planned the crime,
The Great Train Robbery of 1849.

From folk song 'The Great Train Robbery of 1849' by Mike Holgate.

On New Year's Day 1849, an audacious robbery took place on the 6.35 p.m. Plymouth to London mail train. The perpetrators of the crime, Henry Poole and Edward Nightingale, boarded a first-class carriage and during the journey between Exeter and Bristol gained entry to the unguarded mail van and helped themselves to property valued at over £150,000. This was disposed of and never recovered. The crooks then impudently attempted a repeat performance on the return journey. The mail sacks were found to have been tampered with at Bridgewater and, following a search of the train, incriminating evidence was discovered. The pair were then arrested on suspicion and detained at Exeter. The case attracted national interest and featured a banner headline in *The Times*: 'Extraordinary Robbery on the Great Western Railway'.

Edward Nightingale was 'wanted' for another (undisclosed) crime and refused to give his name. He was not identified until the commencement of the Magistrates Hearing at Exeter Guildhall, when Detective-sergeant Edward Langley of Scotland Yard appeared in court and confirmed that the defendant was a 'horse dealer' from Hoxton, London, and well known to the police. Nine months before the robbery, Henry Poole had inherited a fortune and resigned from his job as a GWR guard. According to the *Exeter Gazette*, he took an elegant residence in Exeter with twenty 'superbly furnished' rooms equipped with furniture 'fit for the mansion of any nobleman'. Despite his wealthy lifestyle, Poole could not resist the lure of easy money and gambled his liberty for a treasure trove.

Donning false moustaches and unfamiliar garb – Nightingale wearing a reversible coat of contrasting colours and Poole, a cloak with a high collar and a green felt broad-rimmed hat – the felons put their plan into action at Starcross. After a drink at the Courtenay Arms, they bought one-way tickets on the station and boarded the night train, seating themselves in one of the private compartments of Brunel's spacious broad-gauge first-class carriage behind the mail tender. Poole knew from experience that while the train was travelling between Exeter and Bristol, the guard left the mail van unattended to assist the clerks in the sorting of letters on the adjoining Travelling Post Office. With no stop between Bridgewater and Bristol, there was a window of opportunity of a little over one hour to make their way precariously along the footboards on the outside of the train, using a hook to secure a hold on the top of the carriage, then enter the mail van and plunder the sealed bags containing registered letters and banker's parcels. The heist was a complete success and they disposed of their plunder to the keeping of unknown accomplices at Bristol; then, shortly after midnight, they calmly purchased tickets for the return journey. Greed was to be their downfall; for they could have escaped unnoticed and got clean away in the pandemonium that ensued when the rifled bags were discovered by baffled railway staff.

By coincidence, a passenger on the Bristol to Plymouth train was police superintendent Joseph Gibbons. At Bridgewater, guards informed him that the mailbags had been robbed. Realising that the thieves must still be on-board the train, he ordered a search of the carriages at Taunton. Poole and Nightingale, seated suspiciously with the blinds drawn in a compartment of the first-class carriage, were quickly rumbled when a dozen packages were found under their seats wrapped in a shawl – together with a bundle containing false moustaches, crepe masks, hook, string, candle and sealing wax. When questioned about the booty, both men replied, 'We know nothing about it'.

The thieves returned to Exeter, not as rich men, but prisoners. The key to the failure of their plan was highlighted in evidence given by Leonard Barrett, the mail guard on the 'down' train. He explained that when Poole had worked for the GWR, the oil lamps of the mail van were fixed on the inside of the doorway. Recently, these had been replaced by roof lamps, which made it impossible for the felons to use the candle and wax found in their possession. It was evident that they had intended to light the candle from the lamp and melt the wax to reseal the bags and prevent all possibility of detection until the bags reached their final destination. Instead, the bags were merely re-tied with string and the theft was readily discovered on the outward journey when the train reached Bristol, not London. Without this hitch Poole and Nightingale would have had more time to plunder the 'down' train.

The trial commenced at the Spring Assizes, held at Exeter Castle. The prosecution had insufficient evidence to connect Poole and

Nightingale with the 'up' train robbery, from which valuables were missing, estimated in excess of £150,000. Instead the prisoners faced charges for the theft of a paltry £150 worth of miscellaneous articles from the 'down' train. Nevertheless, when the jury returned a verdict of 'guilty' against both prisoners, the judge showed no mercy in sentencing the pair to be 'transported for fifteen years'.

Ethel Elliot: The Great Pearl Mystery

A lady stayed with her cousin in Torquay,
Denied she had taken her missing jewellery.
Who could predict what the outcome would be,
In the Great Pearl Mystery?

From folk song *The Great Pearl Mystery* by Mike Holgate.

A sensational society scandal, involving an allegation of slander over the strange disappearance of some pearl pendants, came to a dramatic conclusion in the Royal Courts of Justice in London in December 1891, when the judge announced that he had received a letter which may have a significant bearing on the case and that therefore the court was adjourned until the following day.

Earlier, in February of that year, Georgiana Hargreve discovered that some of her jewellery had disappeared from a secret drawer at her villa, 'Shirley', in Torquay. The trick of opening the drawer of the cabinet was known only to a few persons: Mrs Hargreve herself; her husband, retired army officer Major George Hargreve, who at the time was in poor health and abroad at the health spa Aix; Mr Engelhart, a neighbour and friend of the family; and finally, a recent visitor to her home, her cousin, Miss Ethel Elliot, who resided in London. Although the owner of the pearls could not bear to suspect her young relative, who was about to enter into matrimony with Captain Arthur Osborne of the Dragoon Guards, Mr Engelhart offered to make some discreet inquiries. Journeying to the capital, he quickly located the missing gems in a jewellery shop owned by John Spink. He learned that they had been acquired on 19 February from a lady, who received a crossed

cheque for £550 before returning four days later to exchange it for an open cheque. When shown two or three photographs of the suspect by Mr Engelhart, the jeweller confirmed that Miss Elliot was indeed the lady in question, although she had not used that name. Proceeding to the jeweller's bank, Mr Engelhart discovered that the cheque had been cashed in £50 notes issued by the bank and the young lady had gone off with her ill-gotten gains in a canvas bag. Once again, the photographs of Miss Elliott suggested to the clerks the general appearance of the fair filibuster.

The amateur sleuth communicated his painful findings to Miss Elliot's brother, who in turn broke the bad news to Captain Osborne. When he approached his fiancée with the allegations, Miss Elliot demanded to be confronted with her accusers at the jewellers and the bank. She swore that on 19 February she was not within two miles of those places of business, but otherwise engaged in choosing her trousseau in South Kensington. Despite her protestations of innocence, Mr Spink and his assistant, after some hesitation, identified her as the woman who sold the pearls and the clerks at the bank did likewise. Firmly believing his betrothed's alibi, Captain Osborne chivalrously went ahead with the marriage on 5 April, then supported his wife's decision to sue the Hargreves, claiming damages for slander, after the defendants had carelessly aired their suspicions in conversations with mutual friends.

When the case came to court in November, the plaintiff was expecting a child, and won much public sympathy for her situation. There was almost universal belief in her innocence, for no one could understand why an independent woman, with inherited wealth and a generous allowance from her family, should feel the need to steal valuables from a cousin who was also her dearest friend. In the witness box, Mrs Osborne apportioned blame to the defendants, claiming Major Hargreve was in the habit of saying that there was no crime he would not commit for 'oof' (slang for 'cash'). In addition, he was mean and his wife often complained he left her short of money. Perhaps this situation had caused Mrs Hargreve herself to dispose of the pearls – for it was a fact that, in the recent past, she had 'lost' another piece of jewellery which had never been recovered.

The 'Torquay Pearl Robbery' was finally solved when the court re-convened after the mysterious adjournment. In a sensational development, counsel for the plaintiff, Sir Charles Russell, rose and stated that he was withdrawing from the case and under personal instruction from Captain Osborne unreservedly withdrew the unfounded allegations against the defendants, Mr and Mrs Hargreve. The letter received by the judge had been sent by a tailor who had taken one of the banker's notes in question as payment for goods. A £50 note was produced and found to be endorsed by none other than 'Ethel Elliot'. Immediately, a warrant was issued for obtaining a cheque under false pretences and perjury, although the thief avoided arrest by immediately packing several large portmanteaus and fleeing to France. At the end of February 1892, the fugitive voluntarily returned, accompanied by her loyal husband (who had shamefacedly resigned his commission) and a detective inspector from Scotland Yard. Ten days later, after being committed for trial at Bow Street magistrates' court, she pleaded guilty to the charges at the Old Bailey; then, as sentence was about to be passed, the proceedings were remarkably interrupted by her wronged cousin who made a heartfelt plea for mercy on behalf of the sobbing accused: 'I have known her and loved her all my life, and am perfectly convinced she was not in her right mind when she took the jewels'.

Although a sentence of up to seven years' imprisonment was deemed appropriate, the judge, mindful of the disgrace she had suffered and her forthcoming confinement, ordered that the defendant serve nine months 'hard labour'. In the event, Mrs Osborne was not required to give birth to her baby in prison as she was released within two months. Most of her sentence was spent in the medical wing of Holloway Prison and her lenient treatment was hastened by an article in the *British Medical Journal* that noted she had been previously treated for hysteria–epilepsy, a condition where 'there is much disturbance of the mental faculties' leading to 'irregular behaviour' which accounted for her irrational criminal activity. The *Western Daily Mercury*, commenting on the strangeness of the case, commented that, 'The whole narrative reads like one of those compendious works of fiction more especially adapted to beguile a single railway journey, and the solution of the mystery has certainly been as artfully concealed from popular penetration.'

Bruce Reynolds: The Great Train Robbery

The Flying Squad cornered their quarry in Torquay,
Arrested Bruce Reynolds in his villa by the sea.
On the run since 1963,
For the Great Train Robbery.

From folk song 'The Great Train Robbery' by Mike Holgate.

The Great Train Robbery of 1963 was the most audacious heist of the twentieth century and masterminded by Bruce Reynolds. Long before his involvement in the infamous affair, Reynolds had a string of convictions for larceny, receiving, housebreaking, assault and causing grievous bodily harm. In 1962, his gang was suspected of taking part in a daring daylight robbery at Heathrow Airport, stealing a payroll protected by an armoured car. Getaway driver Roy James needed all of his motoring skills, learned from his time as a racing driver, to escape from the scene of the crime in one of two stolen Jaguars. While exiting through a gate in the airport's perimeter fence, he bounced off an Austin A40 trying to block his way, then, once on the main road, he balked traffic in the middle of an intersection, allowing his friend Mickey Ball to catch up and pass through a red light. In the ensuing investigation, Scotland Yard's Flying Squad quickly rounded up James and Ball, suspecting that they had orchestrated the daring getaway. A confession was extracted from Ball, who was jailed, but the case against James collapsed, leaving him free to take part in the next venture.

The airport robbery had netted the gang £62,000, but the same 'firm' set its sights much higher for the next job when leader Bruce Reynolds meticulously devised a plan to hit the Edinburgh to London night train – carrying £2.6million in used bank notes on their way to be destroyed at the Royal Mint. On 7 August 1963, the train was duly stopped by rigging a railway signal located on an isolated stretch of track at Cheddington, near Leighton Buzzard. The cab was stormed and the driver, Jack Mills, coshed over the head after he refused to move the train along the track to the thieves' waiting vehicles. Once, this manoeuvre had been completed by the semi-concussed driver, a human chain was formed to load 150 moneybags onto an old army truck. On this occasion, fast driving skills were not required as Roy James sedately transported some of his accomplices the short distance to a rented farmhouse at the wheel of a Land Rover.

Like a scene from an Ealing comedy, the jubilant crooks counted their ill-gotten gains and passed the time by playing Monopoly with the stolen banknotes – carelessly leaving their fingerprints on the board. When the police located the gang's hideout at Leatherslade Farm, they found an embarrassment of evidence and made short work of rounding up the majority of the culprits. Savage sentences were handed out at the trial of the train robbers, with seven of them – Ronnie Biggs, Gordon Goody, Robert Welch, Thomas Wisbey, James Hussey, Charley Wilson and Roy James – receiving terms of thirty years.

The Great Train Robbery remained hot news, with high-profile prison escapes by Charley Wilson and Ronnie Biggs; criminal mastermind Bruce Reynolds, meanwhile, remained at large before an international manhunt came to an end in November 1968. He served ten years of a twenty-five year sentence after being arrested in a dawn raid mounted by Scotland Yard's Flying Squad on his hideout in Torquay. For the previous two months,

Wanted

1. **Bucks., Aylesbury Co.—ROBBERY.** 3 a.m. 8th inst., at Cheddington, vide Case 42, 22-8-63. Stopped express train, attacked driver, entered travelling post office attached to train and stole 128 post bags containing about 2½ million pounds in currency (about £20,000 in Scottish and Irish notes). **BRUCE RICHARD REYNOLDS,** alias **RAYMOND ETTRIDGE** and **GEORGE RACHEL,** C.R.O. No. 41212-48, b. London 7-9-31, motor

Bruce Richard Reynolds (photograph taken 1960)

dealer/antique dealer, 6ft. 1in., c. fresh (slightly suntanned), h. lt. brown, e. grey (wears horn rimmed or rimless spectacles), fairly well spoken, slight cleft in chin, scar l. eyelid and cheek and rt. forearm. Cons. for larceny, assault on police, receiving, causing g.b.h. with intent, shop, house, workshopbreaking, etc. at Ongar and M.P. (C.O., C-8, C, F, L, P and W). Last. 30-5-63—fined. Is the holder of Passport No. C.206103, issued at Marseilles, France and during the past year has visited Gibraltar, Spain, Monte Carlo, Paris, North Africa. Represents he is in business as an antique

A wanted poster for fugitive Bruce Reynolds.

PRINT CLEARLY   Issued | 9/68 | No.   1166

Surname .HILLER............. Mrs. Mr. Miss   Resident/Visitor

Christian
Names (in full) .KEITH.............................   Filed at

Home Address 29, PENSFORD AVE............ | BM | PN |
.KEW RICHMOND SURREY............. | TQ | GN |
Business Address or School
if resident outside Borough ....

Torbay Address (If visitor) C/O. MARTIN. BRADDONS. HILL RD, E. ... TORQUAY..............................

I agree to comply with the Byelaws, Rules and Regulations of the Torbay Library Service.
Date .11th. Sept. 1968... Signed K. Hiller.............

No. on Electoral List ....

GUARANTEE OVER (To be signed for person not on list)   Form 5/A

Reynold's application for membership of Torquay Library.

the career criminal had revisited the resort where he had spent childhood holidays with his father and step-mother. Accompanied by his wife, Frances, and their six year-old son Nicholas, who attended a private school in the town, the family resided at Villa Cap Martin, a rented luxury hilltop house with panoramic views of Tor Bay. Reynolds planned to move to New Zealand, but after five years on the run, with periods spent in France, Canada and Mexico, his share of the train loot had dwindled from £150,000 to just £5,000. Living the good life, Reynolds and his wife had once quaffed a case of champagne every week but were now reduced to sipping sparingly from a single bottle of vodka. During his stay in Devon, a wave of nostalgia spurred the robber to proudly take his family on a strange pilgrimage to the scene of his greatest crime. He later recalled: 'Standing in the sunshine, staring at the strip of railway line, I explained exactly how the train was stopped, separated and then relieved of its contents. The magic of that night was still with me, even if the money had gone'.

Posing as an antiques dealer, Reynolds's transport was a stolen Lotus Cortina with changed number plates, driven with an insurance cover note and a driving licence issued in a false name. Ten days before his capture, Reynolds had a slight brush with the law for parking too close to a zebra crossing. Although it was only a minor demeanour, a policeman asked him to produce his driving documents at Torquay police station. Although worried, Britain's most wanted man calmly took his son along with him and was not recognised during the routine check. Using an alias, the robber had recently replaced his invalid international licence by taking a driving test at Newton Abbot. He passed – despite his nervousness when the examiner revealed that he had previously spent thirty years as a member of the Flying Squad.

During their brief stay in the holiday resort, the Reynolds family used their current alias, 'Miller', to enrol as members of Torquay Library; the institution later stocked the career criminal's book, *Autobiography of a Thief* – before it was stolen by a disciple!

Chapter Seven

Scandal

Featuring the mutinous career of notorious seaman Captain Bligh, the
sensational downfall of author Oscar Wilde, the match-fixing antics of soccer
international Jack Hillman, the public collapse of Agatha Christie's marriage
and the tragic death of Stephen Ward, used as a political pawn in the
Profumo Affair.

Captain Bligh: Mutiny on the *Bounty*

Awake, bold Bligh!
The foe is at the gate!
Awake! awake! – Alas! It is too late!
Fiercely beside thy cot the mutineer,
Stands, and proclaims the reign of rage and fear.

From poem *The Island* by Lord Byron.

Devonian sea captain William Bligh set out on his ill-fated voyage on the *Bounty* in 1788 to collect breadfruit plants from the Pacific Islands of Tahiti for transplanting in the West Indies. An idyllic life spent basking in the tropical sun and fraternising with friendly native girls unsettled the crew, who were naturally reluctant to return to the harsh rigors of life at sea after their relaxing six-month sojourn on the island. Also, Bligh's unpredictable temper led to personal clashes with his second-in-command Fletcher Christian who complained that he had been 'treated like a dog all the voyage'. The result was an impulsive decision to seize the ship, precipitating the infamous 'Mutiny on the *Bounty*'.

The mutiny on the *Bounty*.

In April 1789, Christian assumed command in a bloodless coup and cast the tyrannical Bligh, together with eighteen loyal followers, adrift in a heavily laden lifeboat. The irascible seafarer, who would be forever mocked, out of earshot of course, as 'Breadfruit Bligh', then proved his worth as a navigator. As befits a man who had served on a pioneering voyage to Australia under Captain Cook, he embarked on an epic journey of survival. Aboard a frail craft, equipped with only a compass and short on rations, the party covered 4,000 miles in six weeks, with the loss of only one life, before reaching safety at Timor, East of Java.

The mutineers, meanwhile, had split into two parties: the majority returned to the paradise of Tahiti, while Christian, realising that the Royal Navy would return to hunt them down, sailed off with eight other seamen aboard the *Bounty* to an unknown destination. In March 1791, HMS *Pandora*, under the command of Captain Edwards, apprehended fourteen of the mutineers on Tahiti and clapped them in irons. The prisoners were held in a cage built on the quarterdeck. Disaster fell on the *Pandora* when it struck a reef passing through the Endeavour Straits. As the sinking ship was abandoned, no order was given to release the prisoners, but a master of arms sympathetically dropped his keys through the bars of the cage, allowing a few to escape drowning. Amongst the four survivors was a young midshipman, Peter Heywood, who had not participated in the mutiny, but had been compelled to remain on the *Bounty* as there was no room in the open boat with Bligh's party. Treated savagely by the shipwrecked officers, eventual rescue brought another ordeal when the prisoners returned to England to face a court martial beginning in September 1792. Following a six-day trial, sentence of death was passed on them all, with a recommendation of leniency for Heywood, who was later granted a full pardon and allowed to resume a successful career in the Royal Navy.

There was no further news of Christian until a remarkable encounter experienced by Peter Heywood in 1808. Late one evening, Heywood, now commanding his own vessel, was ashore in Devonport when a man he immediately recognised as the leader of the mutiny passed him. Quickly turning and calling out Christian's name, Heywood followed him around a corner, only

Pitcairn Island.

to discover that his quarry had completely vanished. A thorough search of the area failed to find Christian, and it was assumed he had returned to England and eluded the authorities.

However, the story took an amazing twist when, that same year, the master of an American merchantman landed at Pitcairn Island and discovered mutineer John Adams, who claimed to be the sole survivor of Christian's party. According to Adams, the group had landed on the island in 1790 with their Tahitian wives and a dozen native male servants. After salvaging what they could from the *Bounty*, the ship was deliberately destroyed by fire to escape the attention of naval patrols with orders to capture the fugitives. Having spent a period of four years on the island, bitter disagreements broke out in the community and one night the Tahitian men attacked and murdered all the Englishmen bar Adams, who was severely wounded. The women then extracted revenge for their husband's deaths by killing all their own countrymen whilst they were sleeping, leaving Adams as the only man on the island with nine women and numerous children fathered by himself and his fellow mutineers.

This being the case, Heywood could not have seen his former shipmate in Plymouth, as Adams's story confirmed that Christian had then been dead for some fourteen years! Indeed, the sighting in Plymouth had taken place almost twenty years after the mutiny; therefore, it was strange that the figure of Christian had apparently not aged, allowing Heywood to make a positive identification. Furthermore, no other vessel had visited Pitcairn Island, so how could Christian have made his way back to England?

Coincidentally, during the year 1808, Fletcher's old tormentor, the villainous Captain Bligh, whose scandalous conduct had embarrassed the navy, faced another mutiny in his capacity as Governor of New South Wales. His highhanded treatment of the military commander resulted in troops marching on Government House and placing him under house arrest for nearly a year, before he was released and exiled to Tasmania. Perhaps, whilst this drama was being played out, the jubilant spirit of Fletcher Christian had returned to haunt the streets of Plymouth – the city of William Bligh's birth!

Oscar Wilde: The Madness of Kisses

Some love too little, some too long,
Some sell, and others buy;
Some do the deed with many tears,
And some without a sigh:
For each man kills the thing he loves,
Yet each man does not die.

From poem *Ballad of Reading Goal* by Oscar Wilde.

Literary genius Oscar Wilde was at the height of his fame in November 1892, when he arranged to stay in Torquay for a period of four months. He leased Babbacombe Cliff from the owner, Lady Mount-Temple, a distant cousin and confidante of Oscar's wife Constance. Her mansion was designed by John Ruskin – Wilde's former lecturer on Florentine Art at Oxford University. William Morris, who named all the bedrooms after flowers, created the interior décor. Oscar worked in the most artistic room in the house, 'Wonderland', which was agreeable to Oscar's aesthetic

Oscar Wilde.

tastes, for adorning the walls were paintings by Pre-Raphaelite artists Burne-Jones and Rossetti. Wilde also relaxed by swimming and sailing with his two sons off Babbacombe Beach. He wrote to Lady Mount-Temple whilst she was wintering abroad: 'I find the peace and beauty here so good for troubled nerves, and so suggestive for new work'.

During his stay, Oscar completed the play *A Woman of No Importance* and made arrangements to publish a limited edition of *Salome*, which had been banned from the stage by the Lord Chancellor because it depicted Biblical characters. In February 1893, he sent a copy to distinguished literary critic and Torquay resident Edmund Gosse: 'Accept it as a slight tribute of my admiration of your own delicate use of the English.' Earlier, Wilde had supervised rehearsals of an amateur production of *Lady Windermere's Fan* directed by the Mayoress, Mrs Splatt, which opened in January 1893 at Torquay's Theatre Royal. He also granted an interview to local history author and solicitor Percy Almy, which appeared in the magazine *The Theatre*. Amongst the topics they discussed were the merits of famous poets; Keats was the absolute 'favourite' of Wilde, Tennyson 'a supreme artist', Shelley 'a magnificent genius' though too 'ethereal'. Wilde had little regard for the work of Robert Browning, nor his wife Elizabeth, who before her marriage had spent three years recuperating from smallpox in Torquay. Almy observed that Wilde had 'an engaging charm' which would win him many disciples and interestingly, in view of the scandal that was about to engulf him, recorded the great man's thoughts on criminals: 'Never attempt to reform a man, men never repent.'

Early in February, Constance left to join friends in Florence. Immediately, Oscar was joined by his close friend Lord Alfred 'Bosie' Douglas, accompanied by his tutor, who wrote of Wilde whilst staying in Babbacombe: 'I think him perfectly delightful with the firmest conviction that his morals are detestable'. The carefree holiday at Babbacombe ended in tears and tantrums when Bosie stormed off after a lover's tiff. Oscar responded with a letter revealing his feelings: 'Bosie, you must not make scenes with me. They kill me, they wreck the loveliness of life. I cannot listen to your curved lips saying hideous things to me... You are the divine thing I want, the thing of grace and beauty; but I don't know how to do it... Why are you not here, my dear, my wonderful boy?'

Two years later, the relationship between Wilde and Bosie was to incite the boy's father, the Marquess of Queensbury, into denouncing Wilde as a 'sodomite'. Oscar responded by bringing an ill-advised libel case against Queensbury in April 1895. Produced in evidence was a damning letter written at Babbacombe Cliff, where Wilde had responded to a poem that Douglas had sent him: 'My boy, Your sonnet is quite lovely, and it is a marvel that those red rose-leaf lips of yours should have been made no less for music of song than for madness of kisses. Your slim gilt soul walks between passion and poetry. I know Hyacinthus, whom Apollo loved so madly, was you in Greek days'. Oscar's case collapsed and he immediately found himself facing criminal charges on twenty-five acts of gross indecency allegedly committed with a number of youths.

Two trials were necessary to decide Oscar's fate, as the jury failed to agree a verdict. During the first, Constance sought refuge from the press at Babbacombe Cliff with Lady Mount-Temple. Whilst there, she wrote a letter seeking guidance from a fortune teller, Mrs Robinson: 'What is to become of my husband who has so betrayed me and deceived me and ruined the lives

of my darling boys?' The lady had already given the answer two years earlier at a party after the London opening of *A Woman of No Importance*. Wilde was noticeably distressed when told that his right palm revealed that he would 'send himself into exile'. Indeed, after serving two years hard labour in Reading Gaol, Wilde fled to France, where his health quickly deteriorated and he soon realised, 'I am dying beyond my means'. Forced to seek accommodation in a seedy hotel which offended his artistic tendencies, he complained prophetically, 'My wallpaper and I are fighting a duel to the death – one of us has to go'. Loyal friends bore the cost of his funeral and one of then complained, with unintended Wildean wit: 'Dying in Paris is really a very difficult and expensive luxury for a foreigner!'

Jack Hillman: A Soccer Sensation

Burnley lost the match and the best team won,
Despite the efforts on and off the pitch
of 'The Burley One'.

Verse by Mike Holgate.

During the early days of professional soccer, a Devon-born football player was accused of match-fixing and bribery in the first scandal to rock the nation's favourite sport. The culprit, Jack Hillman, was born in Tavistock in 1870 and during his schooldays moved with his family to Lancashire. In 1890, his football talent was spotted by Burnley FC, one of the twelve clubs to form the Football League two years earlier.

Quickly establishing himself in the first team, the jocular 6ft, sixteen-stone goalkeeper, nicknamed 'The Burly One', became a crowd favourite and stayed at the club for four years before moving on to Everton, then Dundee in the Scottish League. However, Hillman's stay north of the border was brief as he had his first brush with the football authorities when the club suspended him for 'not trying' and he was sold back to Turf Moor in 1898. Burnley were leading the race for the Second Division league title and in his first home game following his return, Hillman appeared in the club's highest scoring league match, defeating Loughborough 9-3. The opposition's first goal was scored in a bizarre fashion when a clearance by Hillman struck two Loughborough forwards and rebounded into the net, flying past the embarrassed 'keeper.

Despite finishing top of the league, promotion was not automatic for the champions as Burnley had to take part in a newly devised play-off system where the bottom two teams in the First Division each played the two top clubs from the Second Division, home and away, in a mini-league to decide the issue. With one game remaining, Burnley and Stoke City realised that a draw in their match would result in each team winning a place in the top flight at the expense of Newcastle and Blackburn

Jack Hillman.

Rovers. In addition, Jack Hillman, a notorious gambler, had wagered that he would not concede four goals in the four play-off matches. Having already let in three goals, Jack needed to keep a clean sheet to collect his winnings and he played a prominent role in ensuring that a favourable outcome was contrived with a 'gentleman's agreement' to benefit all concerned. The Burnley goalkeeper had once won a bet by not conceding a goal when playing in a charity match with one hand tied behind his back. In this crucial end-of-season decider he could have played with both hands bound and his eyes blindfolded in the match that became infamous as 'the match without a shot at goal'.

The 4,000 spectators who braved torrential rain and a driving wind at Stoke's Victoria Ground soon realised they were watching a farce. The crowd jeered the two teams for their lack of effort and began refusing to return balls when they were booted onto the terraces. The two goalkeepers had a quiet afternoon and were rarely troubled by shot-shy forwards whose rare off-target attempts posed more danger to the corner flags than the goalmouth. It was midway through the first half before Hillman even touched the ball and supporters cheered him sarcastically as he shouted to his defenders to leave the ball that was trickling towards him in the penalty area at a snail's pace.

The *Athletic News* reported: 'The teams could have done without goalkeepers, so anxious were the forwards not to score… The prevailing opinion was that the result would be a goalless draw, and according to – well, prediction – this result was attained'. The Football League reacted to this blatant case of match-fixing by reintroducing automatic promotion and relegation the following season and it would be 100 years before a variation of the play-off system was successfully tried and adopted.

Hillman was rewarded for his part in this sordid affair with the captaincy of Burnley and won his sole England cap in 1899, appearing in the 13-2 trouncing of Ireland. However, a promising international career was abruptly ended by a murky episode that occurred a few months later. In April 1900, Burnley needed to win their last game away at Nottingham Forest to have any chance of avoiding relegation to the Second Division. When the home team won the game 4-0, club officials revealed that the opposition skipper had offered a bribe of £2 a man to the Forest team to 'throw' the match. To compound the scandal, Hillman upped the offer to £5 a head at half-time when his side were down 2-0. Although the rogue claimed he had been only joking, the Football League were not amused by Hillman's antics and suspended him from playing for the whole of the following season.

Transferred to Manchester City in 1902, Jack enjoyed great success when his new club won the Second Division title in 1903 and the FA Cup in 1904, when they were captained by Billy Meredith, one of soccer's immortals and known as the 'Welsh Wizard'. However, controversy continued to dog Hillman when he was suspended for a further eight months for accepting illegal payments from the club in 1906. Having served his 'sentence', he ended his playing career a year later at Millwall.

Despite his record of villainy, Jack Hillman is regarded as one of the great characters in the history of Burnley FC, and following his retirement, he was welcomed back at the club. He filled a coaching role there during the club's most successful period, either side of the First World War, when the team won both the FA Cup and the championship of the First Division. After leaving the game he ran a corner shop in his adopted home town, where he remained a popular figure until his death, at the age of eighty-four, in 1955. In his native county his name stands out alongside the likes of Cliff Bastin of Exeter, Ralph Birkett of Torquay and Trevor Francis of Plymouth, for Jack Hillman was one of only seven Devonian footballers who have had the honour of representing their country at the highest level.

Agatha Christie: The Mysterious Affair at Styles

Agatha Christie, murder in mind,
The English Riviera's Queen of Crime.
The most popular novelist of all time,
The English Riviera's Queen of Crime.

From folk song 'The Queen of Crime' by Mike Holgate.

The atmosphere in the Christie household on Christmas Eve 1926 must have been distinctly 'frosty'. For, although it was Agatha and Archie's twelfth wedding anniversary, the marriage was heading for divorce. Earlier in the month their strained relationship had led to a nationwide hunt when Agatha drove off late at night, leaving behind her wedding ring at the marital home Styles (named after her first novel *The Mysterious Affair at Styles*) in Sunningdale, Berkshire. The world-famous author was embarrassed to find herself at the centre of a murder investigation, in a mystery as baffling as any of her complex works of fiction, when she disappeared for eleven days.

The case unfolded the following morning when Agatha's car was found abandoned, with the headlights switched on, near the edge of a quarry at Newlands Corner, a beauty spot on the Surrey Downs. Thousands of volunteers searched the area looking for a corpse, before hopes for the author's safety were raised when her brother-in-law, Campbell Christie, received a postcard from Agatha saying that she was travelling to an unspecified spa town in Yorkshire. It had been posted shortly after her car had been discovered.

When inquiries in the White Rose County drew a blank, the police in Torquay became involved when they visited the author's birthplace, Ashfield. The villa was derelict and deserted following the recent death of Agatha's mother – a traumatic event that had left her bereaved daughter feeling understandably depressed. However, the press began to suspect that the whole thing was a publicity stunt when Archie revealed that his wife had often said she could disappear at will and no one would be able to find her. He impeded the investigation further by failing to reveal that the couple had argued on the day of Agatha's departure after he revealed that he loved someone else and wanted a divorce. The police only learned of the couple's domestic problems when they interviewed the household servants. Trying to protect his lover, while wondering whether his conduct may have driven his wife to take her own life, the guilt-ridden philanderer became a murder suspect. A week later the pressure was clearly getting to him when he spoke to the *Evening News*:

I cannot account for her disappearance save that her nerves have completely gone, and that she went away for no real purpose whatever. I left home on Friday to spend the weekend with friends. Where I stayed I am not prepared to state. I have told the police. I do not want my friends to be dragged into this. It is my business alone. I have been badgered and pestered like a criminal, and all I want is to be left alone.

9th. December 1926

MISSING

From her home "Styles" Sunningdale in this Division.

Mrs. Agatha Mary Clarissa CHRISTIE

(WIFE OF COLONEL A. CHRISTIE)

AGE 35 YEARS, HEIGHT 5 ft. 7 ins., HAIR RED (Shingled), NATURAL TEETH, EYES GREY, COMPLEXION FAIR, WELL BUILT.

DRESSED—Grey Stockingette Skirt, Green Jumper, Grey and dark Grey Cardigan, small Green Velour Hat, may have hand bag containing £5 to £10. Left home in 4 seater Morris Cowley car at 9.45 p.m. on 3rd. December leaving note saying she was going for a drive. The next morning the car was found abandoned at Newlands Corner, Albury, Surrey.

Should this lady be seen or any information regarding her be obtained please communicate to any Police Station, or to

CHARLES GODDARD, Superintendent,

Telephone No. 11 Wokingham.   WOKINGHAM.

A police description of the 'missing' author.

When Agatha was discovered staying at a luxury hotel in Harrogate, Archie was informed and confronted Agatha in the lounge as she picked up a newspaper bearing her picture. Next day, the *Western Morning News* reported the reunion: 'There was instant recognition... She seemed to regard him as an acquaintance whose identity she could not quite fix.' Archie Christie proffered an unconvincing explanation to waiting reporters: 'She is suffering from complete loss of memory and does not know who she is.' Embarrassed by the critical press coverage, the errant husband felt compelled to write a cheque to reimburse the cost of wasting police time.

The self-inflicted scandal did not diminish the popularity of the author, who went to her grave fifty years later without shedding any light on the matter in her autobiography, which was published after her death. However, in February 1928, she gave an interview to the *Daily Mail* admitting that she had attempted suicide, then a criminal offence, which might have resulted in imprisonment for the author had the police chosen to press charges:

In my mind was the vague idea of ending everything... I went to Newlands Corner... I turned the car off the road down the hill... I left the [steering] wheel and let the car run. The car struck something with a jerk and pulled up suddenly. I was flung against the steering wheel, and my head hit something.

Up to this moment I was Mrs Christie... After the accident in the car, however, I lost my memory... I believe I wandered about London and I then remember arriving at the hotel in Harrogate. I was still muddy and showing signs of the accident... I had a bruise on my chest and my head was bruised.... At Harrogate I read every day about Mrs Christie's disappearance, and came to the conclusion that she was dead. I regarded her as having acted stupidly. I was greatly struck by my resemblance to her and pointed it out to other people in the hotel. I even tried to obtain a book by this Mrs Christie to read.

Whether Agatha hoped that her husband would miss her and end his affair or simply wanted to ruin his romantic weekend and make him suffer embarrassment at the hands of the police is not clear. However, evidence of just how selective a spurned woman's memory can be was brought home forcibly to the unsympathetic Archie when he discovered that his distressed wife had taken refuge in the hotel using the alias Mrs Neele – the surname of his mistress!

Dr Stephen Ward: Scapegoat of the Profumo Affair

Last night he wrote these words to his friend:
'Sorry about the mess,
I'm guilty 'til proved innocent
In the public eye and press.'
The funeral's very quiet because all his friends have fled,
They may be false, they may be true,
But nothing has been proved.

From song 'Nothing Has Been Proved', written by The Pet Shop Boys.

Society osteopath Dr Stephen Ward, a central figure in the explosive sex scandal that rocked the government in the early 1960s, was raised in Torquay and opened his first medical practice in the seaside resort, where his father, Canon Arthur Ward, was the incumbent of St Matthias' church from 1922-1940. During this period, the Ward family resided at a villa that had been the birthplace of rugby union international and war hero Lieutenant-Commander Arthur Leyland Harrison, who was posthumously awarded the Victoria Cross for distinguished conduct, leading a naval raid on Zeebruge in 1918.

During the Second World War, Stephen Ward also answered the nation's call and attained the rank of captain in the Royal Army Medical Corps before returning to civilian life and settling in London. Quickly establishing himself as a leading light in the social life of the capital, he built up an impressive list of wealthy clients, becoming an inveterate namedropper through treating the aches and pains of the rich and famous, including Sir Winston

St Matthias church, Torquay.

Churchill, Elizabeth Taylor, Ava Gardner and Paul Getty. Moving in such high circles, Ward also used his considerable talents as an artist to mount an exhibition featuring portraits of his famous patients and was invited to sketch members of the royal family at Buckingham Palace.

In 1949, Ward became romantically attached to fashion model Patricia Baines, but their marriage was disastrous and lasted just six weeks. It would soon become clear that despite enjoying the company of glamorous women – be they beautiful ladies or high-class call girls – Ward's relationships with the opposite sex became increasingly non-sexual. It transpired that he was a voyeur who allowed his luxury flat in the West End to be used for orgies involving sex and whipping sessions while he looked on, but took no active part. In 1956, he leased Spring Cottage in the grounds of Cliveden, an estate owned by his friend and patient, Lord William Astor, the son of former Plymouth politicians Lord Waldorf Astor and Lady Nancy Astor. During a party held at Cliveden, in the summer of 1961, Ward introduced married government minister John Profumo to topless showgirl Christine Keeler, who had attracted his attention while frolicking naked in the swimming pool. Among the many other men she was sleeping with was a known Russian spy, Captain Eugene Ivanov, causing the society doctor to casually observe there was the potential to start 'World War Three'. Ward had been recruited by MI5 to entrap Ivanov, but it was the Secretary of State for War, John Profumo, who became the first casualty of the scandal. It was the height of the 'cold war', and following press speculation that 'pillow talk' between the call girl, the Tory minister and the Soviet naval attaché might threaten the nation's security, the humiliated politician was forced to resign in March 1963, after lying about his involvement with the woman to the House of Commons, publicly stating that 'There was no impropriety whatsoever in my acquaintanceship with Miss Keeler'.

In an act of political revenge, the Home Secretary, Henry Brooke, then ordered the commissioner of police to investigate the lifestyle of Stephen Ward. Nearly 150 of the doctor's friends and acquaintances were interviewed in an attempt to make him the scapegoat for the sordid affair that had deeply embarrassed the government. Believing that his work for the secret service would guarantee him immunity from prosecution, Ward was surprised to be arrested on the trumped-up charge of 'living off immoral earnings', having supplied members of the social elite with a string of girls for sexual purposes. During the hearings, evidence emerged of a twilight world where famous personages cavorted with young women of loose morals involving drugs, two-way mirrors and black-magic rituals. Appearing as chief witnesses for the defence were Dr Ward's former 'flatmates', twenty-one-year-old Christine Keeler and eighteen-year-old Mandy Rice-Davies (the latter had once rejected a proposal marriage from Ward and was formerly the paramour of notorious slum landlord Peter Rachman). Both girls testified that, although they had received money for their sexual favours, their patron had never lived off their earnings, immoral or otherwise. Ward himself admitted being a 'thoroughly immoral man', but denied he was a 'pimp'. However, the prosecution concentrated on the lurid side that lay behind the prisoner's veneer of respectability. In his closing speech, counsel blackened the defendant's character further, implying it was the jury's patriotic duty to convict the accused. By the time the verdict of 'guilty' was duly delivered, the prisoner, unable to live with the prospect of a term in jail, lay in a coma, having taken a lethal dose of barbiturates and been rushed to hospital halfway through the judge's summing up. The patient never recovered, and a suicide note was found in which he wrote, 'It is really more than I can stand – the horror day after day at the courts and in the streets. It's not only fear – it's a wish not to let them get me. I'd rather get myself... I've given up all hope... I'm sorry to disappoint the vultures – I only hope this has done the job.'

Despite the tragic circumstances of Dr Stephen Ward's death, the most memorable moment of the legal proceedings came when Christine Keeler's friend Mandy Rice-Davis gave evidence. When told that Lord William Astor had denied paying her for sex, she replied disarmingly, 'Well, he would, wouldn't he?'

Chapter Eight

Serial Killers

Examining dubious allegations against the good names of Lady Mary Howard
and Sir Arthur Conan Doyle, the foolish confessions of executed 'witch'
Temperance Lloyd and the annual seaside escapades of the club-wielding
puppet Mr Punch.

Lady Mary Howard: The Black Widow

My ladye hath a sable coach
And horses two and four;
My ladye hath a black bloodhound
That runneth on before.
My ladye's coach hath nodding plumes,
The driver hath no head;
My ladye is an ashen white,
As one that is long dead.

From traditional song 'My Lady's Coach'.

According to legend, when the clock strikes midnight, the ghost of the Old Lady of Fitzford leaves Tavistock in a coach fashioned from the bones of the four husbands she survived. The skulls of her unfortunate suitors adorn each corner of the carriage, which is drawn by a headless horse. Travelling to Okehampton Castle, the cortege is accompanied by a black hound with one eye in the middle of its forehead, which dutifully stoops to pluck a single blade of grass. This nightly ritual, that must continue until the grass no longer grows, is the penance of Lady Mary Howard whom posterity has accused of murdering some of her ill-fated spouses.

Born Mary Fitz at Fitzford Manor, Tavistock in 1596, she was forced at the age of twelve into an arranged marriage with Sir Allan Percy who immediately caught a fatal 'chill' whilst hunting. Aged fifteen, she eloped with Thomas Darcy. His unexplained death occurred a few months after the wedding. Immediately remarrying for a third time, Lady Mary's union to Sir Charles Howard survived ten years before he, too, suddenly succumbed prematurely. Despite this unfortunate track record, the heiress was still looked upon as 'a lady of extraordinary beauty' and 'the richest match in the West' when, in 1628, she entered into holy matrimony with Sir Richard Grenville (1600-1659), namesake and grandson of the naval hero who had lost his life in an engagement against the Spanish on board the valiant *Revenge*.

The bridegroom was heavily in debt as a result of his extravagant lifestyle and obviously regarded this marriage as an ideal opportunity

Lady Mary Howard.

to overcome his financial problems. However, the honeymoon period came to an abrupt end when Sir Richard discovered that his wife had astutely taken legal steps to prevent him gaining control of her riches. Violent quarrels ensued and on one occasion, whilst Lady Mary was expecting their second child, Grenville entered her bedchamber wielding a sword. These incidents brought about an acrimonious divorce and numerous court appearances for Sir Richard, who was ordered to pay crippling fines, alimony, costs and damages leading to imprisonment for non-payment. He was held at 'his majesty's pleasure' before escaping sixteen months later, and sought refuge abroad in October 1633. Despite these misdemeanours, Sir Richard retained the favour of King Charles I and returned from exile in 1639 to take up an army commission, serving with distinction in Ireland. At the outset of the Civil War, he infuriated the Puritans when he hoodwinked them by offering his services to Cromwell, then switching sides once he had received outstanding arrears of back pay from Parliament. His effigy was hung from the gallows and a proclamation denounced Grenville as 'a traitor, rogue, villain and skellum'.

Lady Mary Howard may not have been a serial murderer, but there is no doubt that she was the daughter of one. Her father was the notorious, quick-tempered hell raiser, Sir John Fitz. The wealthy landowner was dining with his friend, Sir Nicolas Stanning of Bickleigh in 1599, when the two men fell out. The drunken Fitz drew a dagger and lunged at Stanning, who blocked the blow with his knife before the antagonists were parted by other guests. Leaving on horseback for his home at Bickleigh, between Tavistock and Plymouth, Stanning was followed by his furious host and four companions. They attacked Stanning, and after a brief skirmish withdrew, with Fitz apparently satisfied that he had avenged the perceived insult. He was then goaded to continue the fight by one of his men who taunted, 'What, child's play; come to fight, and now put up your sword?' Stung into action, Fitz rode back and ran his blade through Stanning. Fleeing across the Channel to France to avoid arrest for unlawful killing, Fitz stayed abroad for several months until his father-in-law, William Courtenay, the 3rd Earl of Devon, of Powderham Castle, intervened and used his influence at court to procure a pardon from Queen Elizabeth.

Riddled with guilt over the death of his friend, Fitz became increasingly dependent on alcohol and was later suspected of killing a police officer during a drink-fuelled rampage. Becoming increasingly paranoid, the knight believed that his life was in danger from the Stanning family bent on revenge. On a journey to London, he grew delusional and angrily demanded accommodation at a public house in Twickenham. Tossing and turning in bed, he awoke and became convinced that his enemies were surrounding the inn. Rushing out of his bedroom in his night-gown, he plunged his sword into the publican Daniel Alley and killed him; he also seriously wounded his wife. When he came to his senses and realised what he had done, the deranged murderer turned the weapon on himself and committed suicide. Dead at the age of thirty, John Fitz fulfilled the prophesy of his father, a keen student of horoscope charts, who predicted when his son was born that he would suffer a violent and untimely end.

Temperance Lloyd: The Last Executed Witch

Witchcraft, that old wicked sin,
Three old crones had dabbled in,
The wretches proudly did confess,
To many acts of wickedness.

Lyric adapted from broadsheet ballad.

The great witchcraft scare that swept through England from the end of the Sixteenth Century was instigated by King James I – nicknamed 'the wisest fool in Christendom'. The sovereign believed in the Divine Right of Kings and, apart from commissioning a new translation of the Bible, wrote a treatise entitled *Demonology* advocating severe measures against witches after experiencing a near-death incident in 1589. While returning home with his new bride, Anne of Denmark, the ship in which they were sailing almost sank in a violent storm. Two women were subsequently burned at the stake after confessing, under torture, that they had used witchcraft to raise the tempest in an attempt to murder the king. The hysteria surrounding witchcraft continued for a hundred years until Temperance Lloyd of Devon became the last so-called practitioner of the black arts to be executed in England.

This celebrated trial of 'The Bideford Witches' took place in 1682, when three destitute beggars, Susannah Edwards, Mary Trembles and Temperance Lloyd, were arrested on suspicion that they had used sorcery. Local people in Bideford claimed that they had been bewitched and suffered harm – such as pricking pains that felt as though pins and awls had been thrust into their bodies – while others claimed that their cattle had died as a result of witchcraft. When questioned, the suspects readily admitted their guilt without facing undue intimidation or torture. All three confessed that they had consorted with the Devil, who had appeared to them in various guises including as a bird, cat or a small black man who had suckled their breasts to draw blood. However, the woman dubbed 'Intemperate Temperance' went even further and, when held at Exeter Goal, she admitted causing several shipwrecks, blinding Jane Dallyn in one eye and the deaths

The Bideford Witches.

of William Herbert, Lydia Burman and Anne Fellow. She seemed to believe that no harm could come to her as she was protected by the Evil One who had urged her to commit murder, stating: 'The Devil met me in the street, and bid me kill, and because I would not, he beat me about the head and back'. It soon became apparent that the 'witches' had been deserted by their master as a pamphlet published at the time relates, 'They also asserted that the Devil came with them to the prison door and there left them'.

Strange marks and unnatural teats, said to have been found on the bodies of the suspects, confirmed their guilt and they were condemned to death. In August 1682, the accused women were conveyed to Heavitree, outside Exeter, where the sentence of the law was to be carried out. After being observed travelling in a cart 'all the way eating and apparently unconcerned', Temperance and her friends arrived at the gallows where they finally seemed to come to their senses. Surrounded by a huge crowd, and berated for their sins by a clergyman, they proclaimed they were innocent of all the charges. However, no one was interested in their last-minute pleas for mercy, and firstly Susannah Edwards, then Mary Trembles were hanged, leaving the person considered the worst culprit to last – in the words of the pamphlet 'the woman that has debauched the other two'. Before the executioner carried out the final act of his grim task, Temperance Lloyd was asked by the Sheriff of Devon whether she believed in God and with her last words she replied, 'Yes, and I pray Jesus Christ to pardon my sins'.

Despite the fact that they had claimed they could only recite the Lord's Prayer backwards, the three 'witches' were granted a request to sing part of psalm forty prior to being put to death. Probably the most appropriate verse being, 'For innumerable evils have compassed me about: mine iniquities have taken hold upon me, so that I am not able to look up; they are more than the hairs of mine head: therefore my heart faileth me'. Fortunately, they were hanged and not burned alive at the stake; this cruel fate had befallen so many other poor wretches suspected of witchcraft, making another verse from the psalm less appropriate for the occasion, 'Sacrifice and offering thou didst not desire; mine ears hast thou opened: burnt offering and sin offering hast thou not required'.

Sir Arthur Conan Doyle: Author of the Perfect Crimes

Sherlock Holmes is on the case,
In the Dartmoor hills.
Trying to solve the mystery,
Of the *Hound of the Baskervilles.*

Verse by Mike Holgate.

Sir Arthur Conan Doyle was born in Edinburgh, grew up in the city and studied medicine before moving to Plymouth in 1882. Joining the practice of Dr George Budd, he resigned after observing the eccentric practices of his employer, who on one occasion insisted that he and Doyle throw plates of food at each other to cure a patient of lockjaw by making the sufferer laugh. During other consultations an old lady in low spirits was told to shake a bottle of medicine and swallow the cork to keep her 'up', while a small child with an irritating cough was cured when

perched upon a mantel-
piece and warned that
one cough would pitch
her into the coal grate
where her skirts would
catch fire. This bizarre
experience provided the
inspiration for the 'bud-
ding' author's character
Professor Challenger,
who insults and bullies his
way through adventures
in *The Lost World* and *The
Land of the Mist*. As for

Sir Arthur Conan Doyle.

Budd's medical methods,
Conan Doyle recalled, 'I have no doubt he did a great deal of
good, for there was reason and knowledge behind all that he did,
but his manner of doing it was unorthodox in the extreme.'

Setting up his own practice in Southsea, Portsmouth, Doyle
created Sherlock Holmes in 1887, and the following year applied
a combination of his own medical knowledge and the cool
logic of his fictional detective to the shocking real-life case of
five murdered prostitutes in Whitechapel. In a letter published
in *The Times*, Doyle suggested that Jack the Ripper might be a
man disguised as a midwife who was able to commit the murders
and walk through the district in a bloodstained apron without
attracting undue suspicion. Conan Doyle himself has been named
as a possible suspect in the hunt for the author of the East End
atrocities, possessing the necessary medical and criminology skills
to fit the profile of Jack the Ripper. The novelist has also been
accused of being implicated in the alleged poisoning of two
well-known personalities. The first case occurred shortly after
Doyle returned from medical service in the Boer War, for which
he was awarded a knighthood in 1902. Tired of the effect that
crime fiction was having on his ambition to become an historical
novelist, Doyle had killed off Sherlock Holmes in 1893, before
bowing to public pressure to revive the detective hero in his best-
known case, *The Hound of the Baskervilles*, written while he was

staying on Dartmoor at the Duchy Hotel, Princetown in 1901. In the book's dedication, the author faithfully acknowledged that, 'This story owes its inception to my friend, Mr Fletcher Robinson, who has helped me both in the general plot and in the local details.'

Journalist Bertram Fletcher Robinson (later editor of *Vanity Fair*) lived on the edge of the moor at Ipplepen and regaled Doyle with local legends of spectral demon hounds. The coachman who drove the pair around the district was the man whose name inspired the title, Harry Baskerville, who later claimed that Robinson had not received the credit he deserved for co-writing the story with Doyle. In 2003, author Rodger Garrick-Steele went further in *The House of the Baskervilles* and presented a theory that Robinson was the sole author of the book, and that he had been murdered at the insistence of Doyle, who, he claimed, was having an affair with Robinson's wife, Gladys; Doyle had persuaded his mistress to administer lethal doses of laudanum to her husband. The symptoms of laudanum poisoning are similar to typhoid, which was the official cause of death when Robinson passed away aged thirty-six in 1907. Doyle, however, curiously contended that his friend, who had dabbled in Egyptology, was a victim of selective poisoning through the same so-called Mummy's Curse that killed Tutankhamun discoverer Lord Carnavon.

Conan Doyle had a child-like belief in the occult, believed in the existence of fairies and was a champion of Spiritualism – an issue he hotly debated in correspondence with Harry Houdini. The legendary escapologist fervently denounced false mediums until his death from peritonitis on Halloween 1926, although his great-nephew, George Hardeen, proposes in *The Secret Life of Houdini* (2007) that no autopsy was carried out on the American showman to determine the cause of death. Furthermore, he contends that it was an act of deliberate poisoning by a group called the Spiritualists, led by Doyle (who wrote to a fellow devotee in 1924 that Houdini 'would get his just deserts very exactly meted out... I think there is a general payday coming soon.').

If indeed Conan Doyle was a serial killer, perhaps he had wanted to prove to himself that he could outwit the law and commit a succession of perfect crimes by utilising the intellect

Doyle has been suspected of being Jack the Ripper.

of his fictional detective outlined in the novel *The Adventures of the Musgrave Ritual* (1931) in which Sherlock Holmes makes a revealing statement: 'You know my methods in such cases, Watson: I put myself in the man's place, and having first gauged the man's intelligence, I try to imagine how I should proceed under the same circumstances'.

Mr Punch: The Seaside Murders

The Punch & Judy Man,
Has a theatre on the sand.
Playing to the crowds,
In the seaside towns,
The Punch & Judy Man.

From folk song 'The Punch and Judy Man' by Mike Holgate.

The loveable rogue Mr Punch is forever popular with children whenever he appears on the beaches of Devon. To the delight of his young audience, he continues to re-enact his catalogue of terrible crimes, clubbing to death his wife, their child, a policeman, the executioner appointed to hang the cunning rascal and, even the author of evil, Satan. Far from being shocked by this spectacle, the thrilled onlookers applaud wildly and reward his behaviour by donating their pocket money to the villain, who sets an appalling example as he wields his weapon and despatches each victim preaching to impressionable young minds: 'That's the way to do it!'

Mr Punch Hanging Jack Ketch
Upon the fatal drop now Punch appears;
Perhaps you're thinking, full of grief and tears.
Not he – the rogue seemed more inclined to joke:
When just as Jack began to fix the rope,
Punch wheeled about, and gripped him in a trice,
Held him as tight as tho' wedged in a vice.
At this old Jack set up a dismal shout –
Pray, Mr Punch, what are you now about!

A Punch & Judy show on Goodrington Sands, Paignton.

Punch tricks hangman Jack Ketch.

Patience, says Punch; don't make such ugly faces
'Tis only you and I exchanging places.
Murder! cries Jack, Dear Jack, quoth Punch, be quiet!
Hang it! You're kicking up a gallows riot!
Quick round his neck the rope bound tight and fast;
Goodbye! says Punch – I've ketch'd him safe at last.

Bibliography and Sources

Chapter One: Murderers

William De Tracy: The Assassination of Thomas Becket.
Baring-Gould, Sabine. *The Lives of the Saints* (London, John Hodges 1877)
Barlow, Frank. 'Becket, Thomas' in the *Oxford Dictionary of National Biography* (Oxford, Oxford University Press, 2004)
Franklin, R.M. 'Tracy, William de' in the *Oxford Dictionary of National Biography* (Oxford, Oxford University Press, 2004)
Hippesley Cox, A.D. *Haunted Britain* (London, Hutchinson, 1973)
Holgate, Mike. *Devon Ghosts and Legends* (Tiverton, Halsgrove, 2009)

Newspapers and journals: *All the Year Round; Illustrated London News; Lloyd's Weekly News; Trewmans Exeter Flying Post; Torquay Directory & South Devon Journal; Western Daily News*

Charlotte Winsor: The Wholesale Child Murderess
The Life and Trial of the Child Murderess (London, *Illustrated London News*, 1865)
Lambert, Richard. *When Justice Faltered* (London, Metheun, 1935)

Newspapers and journals: *Daily Mail; Devon County Standard; East & South Devon Advertiser; Illustrated London News; Lloyds Weekly News; The Times; Torquay Directory & South Devon Journal.*

John Lee: The Man They Could Not Hang
Holgate, Mike and Waugh, Ian David. *The Man They Could Not Hang* (Stroud, Sutton Publishing Ltd., 2005)
Lee, John. *The Man They Could Not Hang* (London, C. Arthur Pearson, 1908)

Newspapers and journals: *Daily Chronicle; Daily Mail; The Graphic; The Times; Mid Devon Advertiser.*

Harry Grant: The Armless Killer

Holgate, Mike. *Murder & Mystery on the Great Western Railway* (Tiverton, Halsgrove Publishing, 2006)

Newspapers and journals: *East & South Devon Advertiser; Torquay Directory & South Devon Journal; Torquay Times & South Devon Advertiser; Western Daily News.*

Herbert Rowse Armstrong: The Dandelion Killer

Holgate, Mike. *Murder & Crime: Devon* (Stroud, Tempus Publishing, 2007)
Odell, Robin. *Exhumation of a Murder: The Life and Trial of Major Armstrong* (London, Harrap, 1975)
Young, Filson (ed). *The Trial of Herbert Rowse Armstrong* (Edinburgh & London, William Hodge, 1927)

Robert Hichens: The Sinking of the *Titanic* Helmsman

Baldwin, Jean. The Book of Manaton (Tiverton, Halsgrove, 1999)
Holgate, Mike. Murder & Crime: Devon (Stroud, Tempus Publishing, 2007)

Newspapers and journals: *Herald & Express; New York Herald; The Times; Torquay Directory & South Devon Journal;, Torquay Times & South Devon Advertiser; Western Morning News.*

Websites: www.encyclopedia-titanica.org

Chapter Two: Smugglers and Pirates

Sir Thomas Stucley: Defamed Throughout Christendom

Gould, Sabine Baring. *Devonshire Characters and Strange Events* (London, John Lane The Bodley Head, 1908)
Gribble, Francis. *Romance of the Men of Devon* (London, Mills and Boon Ltd., 1912)
Holmes, Peter. 'Stucley, Thomas' in *Oxford Dictionary of National Biography* (Oxford, Oxford University Press, 2004)
Hunt, William R. *Rogue's Who's Who* (London, Peter Owen Ltd., 1970)

Francis Drake: Scourge of the Spanish Main

Ellis, Arthur. *A Historical Survey of Torquay*, Torquay, 1930
Gribble, Francis. *Romance of the Men of Devon* (London, Mills and Boon Ltd., 1912)
Kelsey, Harry. 'Drake, Francis' in *Oxford Dictionary of National Biography* (Oxford, Oxford University Press, 2004)
Prince, John. *Worthies of Devon* (London, Longman 1810)

Long Ben: King of the Pirates

David Cordingly. 'Avery, Henry' in *Oxford Dictionary of National Biography*

(Oxford, Oxford University Press, 2004)

Gould, Sabine Baring. *Devonshire Characters and Strange Events* (London, John Lane The Bodley Head, 1908)

Jack Rattenbury: Rob Roy of the West

Gould, Sabine Baring. *Devonshire Characters and Strange Events* (London, John Lane The Bodley Head, 1908)

Gribble, Francis. *Romance of the Men of Devon* (London, Mills and Boon Ltd., 1912)

Rattenbury, Jack. *Memoirs of a Smuggler* (Sidmouth, J. Harvey, 1937)

Chapter Three: Traitors

Lord Thomas Seymour: Protector of the Realm

Bernard, G. W. 'Seymour, Thomas' in *Oxford Dictionary of National Biography* (Oxford, Oxford University Press, 2004)

Holgate, Mike. *Devon Ghosts and Legends* (Wellington, Halsgrove, 2009)

Williamson, David. Debrett's *Kings and Queens of Britain* (London, Webb & Bower, 1986)

Lady Jane Grey: The Nine Days Queen

Froude, James Anthony. *History of England* (London, Park, Son and Bourn, 1856-70)

Holgate, Mike. *Devon Ghosts and Legends* (Wellington, Halsgrove, 2009)

Plowden, Alison. 'Grey, Lady Jane' in *Oxford Dictionary of National Biography* (Oxford, Oxford University Press, 2004)

Williamson, David. *Debrett's Kings and Queens of Britain* (London, Webb & Bower, 1986)

Sir Walter Raleigh: Betrayed by 'Judas' Stucley

Gould, Sabine Baring. *Devonshire Characters and Strange Events* (London, John Lane The Bodley Head, 1908)

Gribble, Francis. *Romance of the Men of Devon* (London, Mills and Boon Ltd., 1912)

Nicholls, Mark. Williams, Penry. 'Ralegh, Sir Walter' in *Oxford Dictionary of National Biography* (Oxford, Oxford University Press, 2004)

Prince, John. *Worthies of Devon* (London, Longman 1810)

Duke of Monmouth: The Pitchfork Rebellion

Froude, James Anthony. *History of England* (London, Park, Son and Bourn, 1856-70)

Harris, Tim. 'Scott, James' in *Oxford Dictionary of National Biography* (Oxford, Oxford University Press, 2004)

Little, Brian. *The Monmouth Episode* (London, T. Werner Laurie, 1956)

Parry, Edward, Sir. *The Bloody Assize* (London, Ernest Benn, 1929)

Chapter Four: Fraudsters

Bampfylde Moore Carew: King of the Beggars

The Life and Adventures of Bamfylde Moore Carew (1745)

An Apology for the Life of Bamfylde Moore Carew (1749)

The Surprising Adventures of Bampfylde Moore Carew (London, A.K. Newman, 1813)

Ashton, John. 'Carew, Bampfylde Moore' in *Oxford Dictionary of National Biography* (Oxford, Oxford University Press, 2004)

Gould, Sabine Baring. *Devonshire Characters and Strange Events* (London, John Lane The Bodley Head, 1908)

Gribble, Francis. *Romance of the Men of Devon* (London, Mills and Boon Ltd., 1912)

Thomas Benson: Crime Lord of Lundy

Gould, Sabine Baring. *Devonshire Characters and Strange Events* (London, John Lane The Bodley Head, 1908)

Chater, J.B. *The History of Lundy Island* (Bideford, Transactions of the Devonshire Association, 1871)

Grose, Francis. *Antiquities of England & Wales* (1785)

Gribble, Francis. *Romance of the Men of Devon* (London, Mills and Boon Ltd., 1912)

Charles De Ville Wells: The Man Who Broke the Bank at Monte Carlo

Holgate, Mike. *Murder & Crime: Devon* (Stroud, Tempus Publishing, 2007)

Lee, John. *The Man They Could Not Hang* (London, C. Arthur Pearson, 1908)

Newspapers and journals: *The Times; Thomson's Weekly News; Western Daily News.*

Maria Fenton: Swindling the Mother of Rex Warneford, VC

Cooksley, Peter. *Air VC's* (Stroud, Sutton Publsihing, 1996)

Gunby, David. 'Warneford, Reginald Alexander John' in *Oxford Dictionary of National Biography* (Oxford, Oxford University Press, 2004)

Times History of the Great War (London, The Times, 1918)

Newspapers and journals: *The Times; Torquay Times.*

Chapter Five: Dartmoor Escapes

William Carter: Death on the Moor

Rhodes, A.J. *Dartmoor Prison* (London, John Lane The Bodley Head Ltd., 1933)

Thompson, Basil. *The Story of Dartmoor Prison* (London, William Heinnemann, 1907)

Newspapers and journals: *Illustrated London News; Penny Illustrated Paper; Trewman's Exeter Flying Post.*

George Whitehead: Joyride to Freedom

Rhodes, A.J. *Dartmoor Prison* (London, John Lane The Bodley Head Ltd., 1933)

Newspapers and journals: *Herald & Express; The Times.*

John Gasken: The Double Escapee

Rhodes, A.J. *Dartmoor Prison* (London, John Lane The Bodley Head Ltd., 1933)

Newspapers and journals: *Trewman's Exeter Flying Post; Western Morning News.*

Frank Mitchell: The Mad Axeman

James, Trevor. *'There's One Away'* (Chudleigh, Orchard Publications, 1999)

Newspapers and journals: *Herald Express; Daily Mirror; The Times; Western Morning News.*

Chapter Six: Robbers

Tom Faggus: The Robin Hood of Exmoor

Blackmore, R.D. Lorna Doone: *A Romance of Exmoor* (London, Sampson, Low, Marston & Co., 1906)

Gribble, Francis. *Romance of the Men of Devon* (London, Mills and Boon Ltd., 1912)

Norris, Gerald. *West Country Rogues and Outlaws* (Exeter, Devon Books, 1986)

Henry Poole: The Great Western Train Robbery

Holgate, Mike. *Murder & Mystery on the Great Western Railway* (Tiverton, Halsgrove, 2006)

Newspapers and journals: *Exeter Gazette, Illustrated London News, The Times, Trewman's Exeter Flying Post.*

Ethel Elliot: The Great Pearl Mystery

Holgate, Mike. *A Devonshire Christmas* (Stroud, The History Press, 2009)

Newspapers and journals: *British Medical Journal; Illustrated London News; The Times; Torquay Directory & South Devon Journal; Torquay Times & South Devon Advertiser; Trewman's Exeter Flying Post; Western Daily Mercury.*

Bruce Reynolds: The Great Train Robbery

Reynolds, Bruce. *Autobiography of a Thief* (London, Corgi, 1995)

Crimes & Criminals (London, W&R Chambers Ltd., 2002)

Newspapers and journals: *Herald Express; Illustrated London News; The Times; Western Morning News.*

Chapter Seven: Scandals

Captain Bligh: Mutiny on the Bounty

Barrow, John, Sir. *The Mutiny and Piratical Seizure of HMS* Bounty (Oxford
    University Press, 1914)
Bligh, William. *An Account of the Mutiny on HMS* Bounty (Alan Sutton, 1981)
Frost, Alan. 'Bligh, William' in *Oxford Dictionary of National Biography* (Oxford,
    Oxford University Press, 2004)
Frost, Alan. 'Christian, Fletcher' in *Oxford Dictionary of National Biography* (Oxford,
    Oxford University Press, 2004)
Laughton, J.K. 'Heywood, Peter' in *Oxford Dictionary of National Biography*
    (Oxford, Oxford University Press, 2004)

Oscar Wilde: The Madness of Kisses

Bentley, Joyce. *The Importance of Being Constance* (London, Hale, 1983)
Hart-Davis, Rupert (ed). *More Letters of Oscar Wilde* (London, Murray, 1985)
Hyde, Montgomery. *Famous Trials 7: Oscar Wilde* (Harmondsworth, Penguin

Newspapers and journals: *Illustrated London News; Penny Illustrated News; The
    Theatre; The Times; Torquay Times & South Devon Advertiser; Torquay Directory &
    South Devon Journal.*

Jack Hillman: A Soccer Sensation

Lee, Edward. Whalley, Phil. *The Pride and Glory* (Burnley, Burnley FC 2002)
Lee, Edward. Simpson, Ray. *Burnley: A Complete Record* (Derby, Breedon Books,
    1991)

Newspapers and journals: *Athletic News; Burnley Express; Devon Life.*

Agatha Christie: The Mysterious Affair at Styles

Christie, Agatha, *Autobiography* (London, Collins, 1977)
Holgate, Mike. *Agatha Christie's True Crime Inspirations* (Stroud, The History Press,
    2010)
Norman, Dr Andrew. *Agatha Christie: The Finished Portrait* (Stroud, Tempus
    Publishing Ltd., 2006)
Thompson, Laura. *Agatha Christie: An English Mystery* (London, Headline Review,
    2007)

Newspapers and journals: *Daily Mail; Evening News; Herald & Express; The Times;
    Western Morning News.*

Stephen Ward: Scapegoat of the Profumo Affair

Davenport-Hines, Richard. 'Ward, Stephen Thomas' in *Oxford Dictionary of
    National Biography* (Oxford, Oxford University Press, 2004)
Kennedy, Ludovic. *The Trial of Stephen Ward* (London, Victor Gollancz, 1964)

Newspapers and journals: *Herald Express; The Times; Torbay Weekender; Torquay Times; Western Morning News.*

Chapter Eight: Serial Killers

Lady Mary Howard: The Black Widow

Gould, Sabine Baring. *Devonshire Characters and Strange Events* (London, John Lane The Bodley Head, 1908)

Norris, Gerald. *West Country Rogues and Outlaws* (Exeter, Devon Books, 1986)

Temperance Lloyd: The Last Executed Witch

Baring Gould, S. *Bideford Witches & Tales of Devonshire Witches,*

Gould, Sabine Baring. *Devonshire Characters and Strange Events* (London, John Lane, The Bodley Head, 1908)

Sir Arthur Conan Doyle: Author of the Perfect Crimes

Gould, Sabine Baring. *Devonshire Characters and Strange Events* (London, John Lane The Bodley Head, 1908)

Edwards, Owen Dudley. 'Sir Arthur Ignatius Conan Doyle' in *Oxford Dictionary of National Biography* (Oxford, Oxford University Press, 2004)

Garrick-Steele, Rodger, *The House of the Baskervilles* (Indiana, USA, Authorhouse, 2003)

Klush, William. *The Secret Life of Houdini* (London, Atria, 2006)

Holgate, Mike. *Jack the Ripper: The Celebrity Suspects* (Stroud, The History Press, 2008)

Thompson, Victor. *Characters and Caricatures of North Devon* (Bideford, Badger Books, 1985)

Mr Punch: The Seaside Murders

Punch and Judy (London, J. Catrach *c.* 1870)

Newspapers and journals: *Lloyd's Weekly News; Trewman's Exeter Flying Post.*

Song Sources

Baring-Gould, S. Fleetwod Shephard. H. Bussell, F.W. *Songs of the West* (London, Methuen & Co. Ltd., 1905)

Crossing, William. *Folk Rhymes of Devon* (Exeter, James J. Commin, 1911)

Eliot, T.S. *Murder in the Cathedral* (London, Faber & Faber, 1935)

Palmer, Roy. *A Ballad History of England* (London, B.T. Batsford Ltd., 1979)

Sergeant, Kitteridge. *English and Scottish Popular Ballads* (London. David Nott, 1904)

Wilde, Oscar. *Ballad of Reading Gaol.*

WANTED

Punch, alias Punchinello, alias Puncinella.
Of Italian origin, speaks with high-pitched squeaky voice.
Distinctive appearance with hunched back and hooked nose.
Wears cap and bells and carries a wooden club.
Escaped from the gallows after hanging the executioner.
Convictions for the murder of his wife, child and a policeman.
Do not approach this puppet – he is armed and dangerous.

Visit our website and discover thousands of other History Press books.

www.thehistorypress.co.uk